Take Heart & Write

How to Pluck Up Courage and Put Pen to Paper

Judy Lawn

DEDICATION

I dedicate this book to writers everywhere.

Also by Judy Lawn

Novels

Progressions

Daisies Never Die

Watch Over Me

TIMEBOY Book One: Gondwana (YA)

The Giant Greglusam (Chapter Book)

Short Stories (Anthology)

Children's Picture Books

The Shrimp Who Wanted to be Pink

Sebastian's Tail

Jossie's New Home

Jamie's Monsters

Non-Fiction

Creative Writing

Judy Lawn

CONTENTS

ACKNOWLEDGMENTS

I would like to thank my family and friends for their wonderful support and encouragement over the years.

Introduction

Eighty percent of people want to write a book, but never begin.

What stops people from taking up their pens?

Take Heart & Write delves into the plethora of problems that stop people from writing, provides solutions, and presents easy-to-follow writing exercises to help writers over those first writing hurdles, to give them the confidence to continue and finish their writing projects.

As a published author with over thirty years' writing experience, and as a creative writing teacher, I have a deep respect for writing.

Students, and those wanting to write, who have struggled with their writing – with even the idea of beginning – have found success by implementing the strategies presented in this book.

Follow the advice and writing exercises presented in *Take Heart &*

Write and overcome the obstacles holding you back from writing.

Don't wait any longer to set sail on your writing journey. Instead of hesitating in the self-doubt arena, step out with confidence and take action now.

The encouragement, writing exercises and tips of the trade you're about to read have been proven to work.

I've witnessed – many times – the pleasure a writer gains from overcoming self-doubt and hesitation to take up their pens.

Why not join them? Take your first steps now and begin your writing journey!

1 FEAR

What Happened at My First Writing Class

My Story

At the first creative writing class I attended I sat with my knees knocking together and my stomach churning. I knew I had to *write* something that my tutor would expect me to read out loud with confidence.

Terror-struck, I shrank in my chair and tried to follow her presentation.

It was like listening to a foreign language.

When she drew this strange symbol on the white board to prompt us to write, I wanted to run from the room.

I stared at the white board like a possum caught in the glare of headlights. What could I write? Her prompt did not inspire me to write.

Everyone else was writing and this only added to my distress. My gaze dropped to my blank page – no help there. All I could feel was the fear coursing through me. What was I doing here? Why had I ever imagined I'd be a writer? I'd never write anything!

Eventually, after long agonizing minutes, I scribbled a few words on my page – long since lost in the passage of time, thank goodness.

The only thing that saved me from mortification was the fact that I was one of the last to read out my work. By this time I'd absorbed some of what the other writers had said, and formed a better understanding of what I could have written. I mumbled my few words and hoped I didn't appear a complete loss.

In hindsight it's easy to recognize I'd allowed my fear to take control, to paralyze my imagination, to all but destroy my

enthusiasm and eagerness to learn.

No wonder I'd found it almost impossible to write.

I had to discover ways to cope with my fear, to find my 'writing

feet', my courage and confidence.

Anyone can learn to do this; to take that first extraordinary leap

into the unknown.

Fear

Most people fear a new experience; there's no certainty of how

the experience will play out, no certainty of achieving the results

we want.

There's only our raw fear.

Wikipedia states that, 'the emotion, *fear*, has been hard-wired into almost every individual, due to its vital role in the survival of the individual'.

If we didn't experience fear we'd walk straight into a forest fire or a raging river or into the path of a dangerous animal.

- ✓ Fear is there to protect us.
- ✓ Fear is on our side.

Over the years I've learnt to put in place ways of dealing with my fear.

I joined Toastmasters, even though the idea of speaking in front of an audience terrified me. Imagine my surprise to discover others suffered a similar fear.

Joining Toastmasters turned out to be a rewarding experience. I was able to share strategies with other members for coping with anxiety, to joke and laugh about our nerves – albeit nervously!

Even the most experienced of public speakers will attest to feeling nervous before a major speaking engagement. It's normal.

Without that nervousness singing through our veins and urging us forward we'd never have the courage to step upon the stage.

So remember, fear is part of our make-up.

Why do new writers fear to put themselves out there in the writing field? Is it the fear of rejection, both personal and professional? The frightening thought that no one will like you or your books?

The expectation that everyone will like us and our books is not realistic.

But that's not a bad thing. Imagine if everyone in the world liked you and your books – you'd never have a minute's peace. People would pound on your door night and day demanding interviews, autographs, books, and your inspirational theories on everything. To me, that's terrifying.

A more realistic expectation is that many people *will* like you and your books; and that can be one of the most rewarding aspects of being a writer.

Surely you won't hold back now because of natural fear? Imagine your friends and family, and even strangers who'd love to read your books? Don't disappoint them.

You want to write. Don't let fear stop you.

Courage

'Courage is the ability to do something that frightens us.'

(*Reader's Digest Word Power Dictionary* 2001)

To cope with your fears and the things that stop you from writing, you need to understand this from the outset.

Courage is the opposite of cowardice. It is: bravery, guts, daring, nerve, audacity, pluck, valor, and the ability to act on your convictions.

You have every one of these capabilities. Sometimes you need to dig deep to find them, to allow them to rise to the forefront of your mind, to remind you that you *can* achieve whatever you set out to do.

Armed with this knowledge, you can't fail. You've taken the first step, picked up your pen, fronted your computer, and now you're ready to begin.

Courage is your armor plating. With your 'armor of courage' you're ready to face whatever challenges cross your path.

Again, it's not realistic to think there won't be challenges along the way. There *will* be. Times when things don't go right, when everything you write seems inconsequential and even rubbish. Accept that those moments will happen.

It's part of writing.

You have within you the courage to work through these tough times, to prevail. No obstacle, no matter what, will prevent you from continuing with your writing journey because of your courage.

I wish I'd understood from the beginning the power of courage.

You need to roar your challenge like a lion, not hide away like a timid mouse, too frightened to write.

Try repeating the word, 'courage', to yourself like a mantra; courage, courage, courage.

Metaphorically, pin the badge of courage to your chest every day before you write and there will be no stopping you.

Your Writing Journey Begins

Patience

Every journey begins with the first step. If you've decided you want to write – you've already taken that step.

Don't give in to impatience, or worry there's too much to learn and that you'll never find the time, energy or the ability to absorb it all. Have patience. You're more capable than you think. You *will* achieve all you set out to do.

Patience was something I had to learn in those early writing days. I wanted things to happen faster than they were. I wanted to write faster, hear from publishers sooner and see my work in print – now. I grew frustrated and allowed my impatience to take precedence, to interrupt and block my writing.

Don't allow this to happen to you.

Imagine yourself on the 'writing highway'. There will be stretches of straight road where you can travel at top speed. 'Road works' will force you to sit and grit your teeth and follow along in the lines of traffic until you're in the clear again. Other unforeseen obstacles confronting you will interrupt your journey. Your vehicle might break down and you'll be forced to wait for help.

Take it all in your stride and don't allow obstacles to stand in your way.

Writer Zone

- Relax and allow yourself to become immersed in your writer zone.

- Listen to music or try deep breathing exercises.

- Get yourself a coffee and chocolate biscuits – whatever works to empty your mind of daily clutter and get you into the writer zone/mood.

- Say, 'I'm beginning my writing journey today'.

- Be *specific* not general.

- 'Today I begin a new journey' is general. 'Today I begin my new writing journey' is specific – and inspirational and encouraging.

- You've found the courage to begin, and that's your first step.

I can hear you saying, 'It's all right for her, she's been writing for years and has gone through the difficult stages. But where do *I* begin?'

That's a stressful thought returning to clutter your mind, and it's time to move away from stressful thoughts and clutter. Take a moment to reclaim your writer's mind, to find your way back to your writer zone. You need to be in the 'write' frame of mind to absorb the next section, enthusiastic and keen to start.

What I Did When It Was My Turn to Teach Creative Writing

Plus: Your First Writing Exercise

I never forgot my first writing experience — that almost disaster day!

Years later when I taught creative writing myself, I set out to ease my students' fears from the beginning.

I always greet my students cheerfully as they arrive, introduce everyone, and ask them about their writing and writing aspirations. I pass around my own books for them to glance through as everyone is arriving and settling. We discuss books they've read or want to read and the latest blockbuster films.

I get them laughing as soon as I can by using a 'joining-in' session as my first writing prompt. This is to describe someone's eyes/features, and how their character's expressions change according to their mood or circumstances. I suggest they avoid clichés: heart-shaped face, furrowed brow, square chin, animated expression etc. When a student asks, 'How many words do I have to write?' I always say in a casual tone, 'Oh, one or two sentences, a couple of paragraphs, six pages'. This brings a few chuckles, and I can sense everyone relaxing.

I don't force my students to read their work out loud on that first day. I ask, 'Who feels brave enough to read out one or two words describing their character's features without giving away gender'. There's always that brave soul who starts the ball rolling.

Then, as a class, we try to work out whether their character is male or female by studying the words each writer has used. This gets everyone joining in and creates a few laughs when I get it wrong. They then see me as a person, not the fearsome teacher. The exercise helps students hurdle that first fear barrier. They can then relax and write with more ease.

Exercise One

- Use this exercise as your own 'writing beginning'.
- Read your partial sentence to your partner/work mate/sibling and see if they can guess the character's gender.
- Study the words you've used. Are words gender related? Do we use different words to describe our characters?

- Write both a male and female character and compare your two pieces – so that's two exercises.

Example One

...voice – high, light, as feathery as the wind through the trees ...

Is this a male or female character? Why? Try to guess the character's age. Below is the sentence in full.

Her voice – high, light, as feathery as the wind through the trees – was another surprise.

(Excerpt from my novel, *Daisies Never Die. Zumaya Publications* 2005, 2011)

The character is an older woman.

Example Two

...eyes were gray and cold and dead...

What is your reaction to this excerpt? Is the character male or female? Why?

Below is the sentence in full.

His eyes were gray and cold and dead, lacking even the usual grimness I'd expected.

Analyze the words used in each sentence. We tend to use harder and harsher words to describe men and softer words to describe women; although it's not a rule set in stone. It depends on the story you're writing, and your character.

Examine how other writers describe their characters in the books you read.

Exercise Two

- Try the exercise I mentioned earlier.

- Find a photograph of an unusual symbol.

- Study the symbol for several minutes then begin writing.

- It may work for you. We're all different.

- Some ideas work better than others.

To Re-Cap What We Covered in Chapter One

* What Happened at My First Writing Class

My Story

* Fear

Fear is on your side.

* Courage

Courage is one of the most powerful tools in your writing kit.

Metaphorically, pin the badge of courage to your chest every day before you write and there will be no stopping you.

* Your Writing Journey Begins

Every journey begins with that first step.

* Patience

Have patience. You're more capable than you think. You *will* achieve all you set out to do.

* Writer Zone

Relax and allow yourself to become immersed in your writer zone.

* What I Did When It Was My Turn to Teach Creative Writing

* Plus Your First Writing Exercises

Exercise One and Two.

2 REWARDS

In Chapter Two we cover a lot, beginning with the power of reward and encouragement, and the importance of knowledge and learning.

I talk about the changes in the publishing world, and there are sections on practice, determination, accountability, discipline, routine, perseverance and focus.

Exercise Three uses sentences as writing prompts.

Rewards

Congratulations! You've written something, completed the first writing exercises.

Reward yourself with a huge mental pat on the back – or chocolate if chocolate is your thing. It works for me.

Give yourself a reward at the end of every writing session, your first paragraph, your first page, the first chapter of your novel.

- Print the pages out and frame them.

- Pin each completed exercise to a cork board and hang the board above your writing desk.

- Put gold stars/pink hearts on your pages.

- Find photographs to go with your stories.

- Read your work to your family/friends/colleagues and ask for *honest* feedback.

- Post your work on social media sites. Invite people to join your writing journey.

- Write a blog detailing why you began your writing journey and what you want to achieve.

- Watch your writing – and your confidence – grow.

The Power of Reward and Encouragement

The above might sound a shade juvenile, but think of it as encouragement, a fun way to congratulate yourself upon completing your first writing assignments.

Never underestimate the power of reward and encouragement in the creative field. Reward yourself, and take pleasure in your achievements.

On those 'doubting days' your framed written pieces, gold stars and photographs on your cork board will remind you of your accomplishments.

Read through your blog again. Add another entry, detailing how stuck you are at present and what you plan to do to get over this hump. It'll be fun reading again at a later date – plus you'll have written something and achieved your writing goal for the day.

Sentences

Sentences are great writing prompts; one sentence leads to another as they say.

For Exercise Three, start with a sentence and see where your writing takes you. Continue on with what you began in Exercises One and Two, or try a new sentence.

Your writing challenge for this exercise is to start writing and keep writing until you finish.

It's time to 'take the bull by the horns' and dive in.

Exercise Three

- Do those two clichés bring a picture to your mind? Great – see what a short sentence can do?

- Write several paragraphs describing diving into the sea/pool or taking the bull by the horns – literally or figuratively.

- Make the paragraphs funny/ridiculous/serious. The main thing is to write.

- Describe the sea/pool/bull/scenery, and your character.

- If it helps, find a photograph of the sea/pool/bull.

- Write your piece first before you read my example.

- Good luck.

Example:

It was the biggest pool the boat possessed, but Marilyn didn't let that faze her as she dived into its cool turquoise depths. This was her first cruise, her first swim, and she didn't want to waste a moment.

The lithe, sun-browned body effortlessly completing laps, water sluicing off his powerful shoulders, had nothing to do with her choice. She was here to enjoy her holiday, and she wasn't

going to let her ex-husband deter her from her aim. If she

bumped into him while swimming, or later in one of the bars

she'd glimpsed on her way to the pool, well, she'd cope.

Pulse racing faster at the thought, she bounced to the surface,

shook the water from her eyes and lifted her face to the warmth

of the sun.

The Results

If you tried the swimming pool idea first, move on to a short piece

about a bull. Remember your bull is a character.

Examine both pieces. Which do you prefer? Why?

Practice and Determination

Practice is one of the best things you can do to improve your writing. Make time for practice writing sessions as often as you can, every day if possible.

You want to write, right?

Use all the exercises in *Take Heart & Write* as practice, or invent your own.

Be determined.

You Need to be a Reader

If you want to be a writer, you need to be a reader. I've been an avid reader my whole life; reading is one of life's joys.

If you've chosen to write in a particular genre, it pays to read what's being written and published in that genre. Search out the bestsellers in your local library, bookshop or on-line.

Knowledge and Learning

From the beginning I realized I needed to learn *how* to write. So, I embarked on what I now refer to as my 'study years', which continue to this day. I completed several English papers through Massey University New Zealand, a course on Creative Writing, and Journalism – all by correspondence.

I also joined the first in a long line of local writing groups and writing organizations.

Completing assignments, writing to a deadline and taking exam papers was good for my writing discipline, if not for my nerves! I gradually gained experience and knowledge and my confidence as a writer grew.

We learn by doing. It's a simple formula but effective.

I can't stress enough how important it is to learn your craft, and to mix with like-minded people. Knowledge is knowledge for life. But interaction with other keen writers is great for your writing soul and a terrific way to keep you motivated. It's also a good way to meet and make new friends – once a writing friend, always a writing friend.

Today, it's so much easier with the wonderful choice of writing groups on social media. But join your nearest local writing group. You'll find a bunch of people willing to talk about writing all day long and share their industry knowledge.

The writer's world is often solitary, so interaction with others, those who understand, is vital.

Other Writers' Journeys

Other writers' journeys make for fascinating reading and

illumination. To discover that others suffered from the same writing nerves and doubts as I did was a relief to know – I'd assumed I was unique.

When you realize you're not alone, you can reach out to others. Family and friends understand how important your writing is to you, other writers will, too.

Most of the writers I've known over the years are prepared to help new writers, to pass on what they've learnt from their own experiences.

Published Works

The publication of my first short story was a huge boost to my confidence and self-esteem as a writer – and the single biggest thing at the time to help me conquer self-doubt. At last I was in print! I was so thrilled I had the story framed.

Over the years, other short stories followed, then my children's picture books and novels. I joined a small local newspaper as editor, and published many profiles, articles and advertorial pieces.

Publication is validation for most writers.

Times Have Changed

But the publishing world has changed.

You don't need to wait for months and months for your stories or books to be published. You can publish on-line, or via social media and blogs the moment you've finished writing them. No longer do you have to publish through traditional channels to become a published author.

This has unlocked a world that didn't exist thirty years ago when I first started writing; a world that writers, entrepreneurs, teachers and artists have embraced.

I can only imagine how this might have helped me when I first began writing; how it must help first time authors today. You guys are so lucky!

There's so much more help for authors than there ever was. Experienced writers, creative writing tutors and entrepreneurs offer dozens of on-line courses, some of which are free.

The past is the past; it's a new beginning in the writing world.

Be excited; there's never been a better time to write!

An Artist's Journey

An artist I knew wanted to paint. Painting was a new field for him, but he was determined to launch his career and achieve success.

So he began. His first painting he threw away. Ditto the second, third and fourth paintings and dozens more.

But with each painting he completed he improved his technique. He saw his landscapes, seascapes and subjects take shape, and understood in more depth the medium he was working in. He asked other artists how they achieved perspective, what colors they were never without on their palettes, and studied other artists' works so he might improve his own paintings.

It wasn't long before the artist held his first exhibition. Soon he was exhibiting and selling his works at major galleries and exhibitions throughout the country.

His determination had worked. He never allowed disappointments to stand in the way of realizing his dream.

You can apply this same principle to your writing.

Don't throw away any of your writing as you might use/need it later.

(See section on writer's block.)

Keep in mind the principle of practice. The more you practice the better you'll be. Practice makes it perfect.

So practice, practice, practice!

Accountability, Discipline, Routine and Perseverance

Every one of these has helped me overcome my doubts as a writer.

Self-accountability is a powerful motivation; you and you alone are responsible for your writing. You can talk about your desire to write, and discuss your book in detail with others, but only *you* can write it.

This leads on to routine and discipline. Impose an everyday discipline of writing; it gets you writing and keeps you writing. From here you'll soon find the routine that best suits you and your lifestyle.

Perseverance is the golden crown that sits upon your head as you write.

Perseverance.

Focus

I couldn't leave this chapter without mentioning focus, and how important focus was to get me past the tough spots and doubts in those early days.

I had to learn how to give each writing session my full attention and not let my mind wander away from the task at hand.

When I started my writing career I didn't own a computer – yes, it was that long ago. I soon got one though, and what a miracle it seemed after bashing away at typewriter keys and using 'type-out' to erase mistakes.

While some writers can't face distraction of any kind when writing, others can write while listening to music, or even in a busy café.

I once thought I needed complete peace and quiet before I could write and wrote for many years in this 'sacred environment'. Now I write with the radio on, in noisy suburbia.

Learn to block out distractions and background noises to focus on your writing so it becomes your center of attention, your 'focal point'.

Without focus you'll never begin your writing project, progress through it, or finish it.

Successful People

Successful people achieve success because they have determination and the ability to stay the course no matter the obstacles they find in their path. They're determined to succeed. To give up or give in never occurs to them.

Anyone can quit. You don't even need an excuse.

It's more difficult to stay the course. This is where focus and determination play their part. Embrace them. Give yourself a daily pep talk, or plot a daily performance chart. Tick off tasks as you complete them to help keep you on track and enthused.

Dreams and Aspirations

It's difficult to stick to your dreams and aspirations when the going gets tough, but this is where you need courage, your *heart*. By looking deep within your heart and mind, you *will* find the answers and a way through those difficult phases.

By labeling them as phases, or a stage you're going through, it reduces them to something manageable.

Let nothing stand in your way. Allow your dreams and aspirations to be foremost in your mind as you begin your writing journey.

Truth and Honesty

You need to be truthful with your 'writer self'; to regard your writing with honest eyes.

As you progress you'll learn to recognize what works and what doesn't.

Other Helpful Advice to Keep You in the Writer Zone

* Verbal Affirmations

Tell yourself you're doing well – encourage yourself as you write;

verbal affirmations are a powerful tool.

* Lists of Achievement

Make a list of the exercises and tick them off as you complete them. This is another powerful tool many creative people use to great effect.

* Ask For Support and Encouragement

Ask your family/friends/work colleagues to offer encouragement; don't forget to thank them for their support.

To Re-Cap What We Covered in Chapter Two

* Rewards

Give yourself a reward at the end of every writing session.

* The Power of Reward and Encouragement

Never underestimate the power of reward and encouragement in the creative field.

* Sentences

Use sentences as writing prompts.

* Practice and Determination

Practice makes it perfect. Be determined. Stick at your writing projects.

* You Need to be a Reader

Writers need to be readers.

* Knowledge and Learning

Make learning a lifelong apprenticeship.

Join your local writing group.

* Other Writers' Journeys

Read other writers' journeys for inspiration.

* Published Works

Publish your writing from the beginning – for your family; publish on-line, or with traditional publishers.

* Times Have Changed

Times have changed in the publishing world.

* An Artist's Journey

Determination wins through.

* Accountability, Discipline, Routine and Perseverance

Be accountable to self. Be disciplined and set yourself a writing routine. Persevere.

* Focus

Stay focused on your writing. By staying focused you'll begin, proceed and finish your writing project.

* Successful People

Successful people succeed because they stay the course no matter what.

* Dreams and Aspirations

Allow your dreams and aspirations to be foremost in your mind as you begin your writing journey.

* Truth and Honesty

Always be truthful with yourself.

* Other Helpful Advice to Keep You in the Writer Zone

Verbal affirmations, lists of achievement, asking for support.

3 THE POWER OF WORDS

In Chapter Three the writing exercises use 'keywords' as a writing prompt. Never be stuck for words, inspiration is everywhere.

There are tricks of the writing trade, ways to save your ideas, and a section on writer's block. I also discuss success and inner belief.

Inspiration

It's easy enough to write a sentence or two, but how do you progress from sentences to write the first pages of your book?

Remember the blank page in the first chapter? Or is the white computer screen holding you back. There's no inspiration in empty spaces. You need to fill those empty spaces with words.

Those words need to inspire. They need to take your readers on a journey.

You don't want to write a boring book or bore your readers. You need words that are inspirational/thrilling/moving, thousands of them.

Take Heart – have confidence in yourself. *Focus.*

Inspiration is everywhere – in the familiar world around you, your travels, work place, favorite café, books, magazines, TV shows and the internet. The possibilities are endless. You will never run out of inspiration.

Words

Wouldn't it be great if you could go to the supermarket and buy several thousand words and know those words were the ones you wanted?

And what if there was a simple recipe you could follow to write your books?

Some writers can produce a book in a week/month. To write a book that fast requires a great deal of planning before the actual writing process begins.

With audio transcription now available, writers record their books and have them transcribed – so the writing process is speeding up.

But back to those words – you need to *make every word count*. Your words are important; not randomly chosen and strung together in a haphazard fashion. That's not the way writing works. The words you need for your books require a great deal of thought. But don't panic – select the words you need and discard those you don't need.

Exercise Four

- Study the following list of words.

- Envisage the whole picture they present, rather than noting each word separately.

- Let your mind be free of life's clutter and concentrate on the words.

- Do you see a picture emerging?

- Write a snap-shot scene of several paragraphs.

- Take your time and relax. It's not an exam or a test.

- The list of words is a prompt to help you along your writing journey.

- Again, don't be tempted to read my example before you begin your own.

tree, emptiness, silence, lion, pelt, grass, heat, shimmer, desert, zebra, black and white, haze, mirage, fly, manure, elephant, golden, dust, gray, cloud, sunlight, reflection, midday, light, picture, creature, tall grasses

Did a picture soon form in your mind? The word 'lion' might have given you an idea.

Now read through the list again and begin writing.

- Use your senses: sight, sound, taste, touch and smell.

- Your task in this exercise is to include a reference to smell. It can be a direct reference: 'the plains smelt of wild game' or something subtle like: '... settling in the dry dust once more with a puff'.

- Ask questions. Where am I? What's happening? Will the wild animals charge? Anything that prompts an answer will always get you writing.

- Imagine yourself or your character in the scene.

- Good luck.

Example:

I had watched the lion under the tree for the best part of twenty minutes. It was hard not to be in awe of such a magnificent creature, lying among tall grasses the same tawny gold as his pelt.

Now and then his tail would lift and swish at an unseen midge or fly before settling in the dry dust once more with a puff. Even as I watched, he opened his jaws in a wide yawn, showing off impressive canines.

King of the beasts he was! Lord of all he surveyed! How effortlessly he kept elephant, zebra and other herd animals at a respectable distance from his sunlit slumbers. None dared trespass upon the King's territory.

I wondered if he knew of our presence. The thought caused a shiver of nerves to tighten my skin. Perspiration dampened my forehead. I was suddenly glad of the vehicle. It blocked the burn of the sun – and kept the King of beasts at bay.

Slowly, slowly, as if I might disturb that mighty giant, I lifted my camera.

You can bring a scene to life in a few paragraphs.

Keep referring to your list of words. Use each one to prompt you to write the next sentence, and then the next, until your snapshot scene is finished.

Exercise Five

- Let's try another list of words. Read through them and take a few minutes to gather your thoughts, to allow a picture to capture your senses.
- Use the same questions as in the above exercise, and all the senses – don't forget smell.
- This time, try to write the scene from start to finish if you can; a scene, with things happening – action! That is your writing task for this exercise.
- Once again, begin your own piece before you read my example.

sea, waves, swimmers, bright, sunny, white, glare, heat, sand,

shells, bucket and spade, children, seagulls, towel, sunscreen,

umbrella, beach bag, surf ski, seaweed, driftwood, sand fly, dog,

people, log, foam, flotsam, shoreline, tide, river, sunshine, people,

noise, excitement

Example:

What a relief to reach the beach! Over the children's excited

chatter, we gathered tents and towels, buckets and spades and

other beach paraphernalia and stumbled, drunk on sunshine and

holiday bliss, to the blessed hot sand. It didn't matter that

everything landed in a jumbled heap at my feet or that I was the

one expected to right it all; we'd arrived, the day was ours.

My husband shucked his town clothes like a snake shedding its

skin to reveal bright board shorts. The children crammed

themselves into togs and bikinis with squeals of excitement, and

reached for surfboards, flippers and face masks with such blasé abandon I wondered how we'd managed to pack it all in the car.

When they'd gone I sank to my towel, taking a moment to wriggle my body into the warm sand beneath me and stretch out my town legs to the sun. I allowed a long satisfied sigh to drift out and mingle with the noise of other beachgoers and the ever-present music of the waves.

I closed my eyes and took a deep breath of salty air. For now this was mine and mine alone. I was free of wifely/motherly chores for a good while. I wouldn't think of dripping shivering cranky children who would soon encroach upon my solitude, squawking for food like hungry seagulls.

That was later. This was now.

Keywords

These word lists are called 'keywords'. They're a great way to gather your thoughts or ideas for a story, if you haven't as yet decided on a way to begin. By using keywords to paint a picture of your scene you'll at least have something down on paper/computer screen.

You might use all the words in your story, or just some of them. The choice is yours.

The idea is to find words. It's not as difficult as you think – or as frightening. Build a word platform, a springboard to launch your writing career.

Or call it your word bank; every word you write is one more word in your word bank. Imagine your bank increasing and expanding as you practice writing. Every day you're harvesting more words to store in your bank. Your confidence and faith in yourself as a writer is growing.

There are millions of words; you will never run out.

Write At Your Own Pace

Don't be concerned about what anyone else is doing. It can be overwhelming and even intimidating to read that another writer has written four books in a month, or has thirty books to their credit, and after only a few short years of writing. Remember, you're not allowing negative/worrying thoughts to crowd your mind. You're staying positive, and in your writer zone.

I'll use a walking analogy here. You walk at your own pace. If you're conscious of adjusting your pace to other walkers, this thought stays foremost in your mind. It crowds out your creative ideas – in this case your writing.

Write at your own pace.

Productivity

Some days are more productive than others; that's the way of writing. Don't be disillusioned by the less productive days. Keep writing and remember your book is building word by word, sentence by sentence, chapter by chapter.

Sometimes that finish line can seem a million miles away. Other days you can see it plainly. Keep your focus on your present pathway and try not to be sidelined by obstacles.

There *will* be obstacles. Imagine them as stones or boulders. Plenty are small and easy to step over, others you'll haul yourself over with effort. But get over them you will.

I often noted in class that some writers wrote faster than others. I fall into the slow category, so I knew my fellow slow writers worried about their inability to write faster. I always tried to reassure them that we write at our own pace.

It's not a competition.

It's about writing at your own pace and being satisfied with what you've written.

Creative Time

Work out your most creative time. Are you an owl or a lark? I'm a morning person and that's when I write. Afternoons and evenings are reserved for reading emails or housework. Don't waste your most creative hours on mundane tasks.

Tricks of the Trade and Safety Nets for Your Ideas

When I get stuck on a chapter or can't think of the exact word I need, I take a break. I get up and walk about the room or make a cup of tea. My mind is still focused on my story and it's not long before the word I want floats into my mind, or I realize how I can proceed.

It's all about finding the tricks of the trade to keep you on track. You'll soon find those that work best for you.

Stop each writing session in the middle of a paragraph/chapter. The following day when you read through it again, you can carry on without hesitation. If you want to add something before you sign off for the day, write several keywords or headings on the same page so you have a 'heads up' for your next writing session.

This is a safety net for your ideas. Keywords and headings will trigger your memory. It's all about saving your ideas, having leads and being able to keep up the flow of writing.

By doing this, you'll rarely be stuck in your writing; your thinking will be clearer and your writing will flow.

Writer's Block

You may have heard of writer's block. You may even laugh.

But writer's block is no laughing matter. I know, because I've suffered and so have other writers.

Writer's block happened to me years ago.

I'd come to 'the end of my writing', the realization that I wasn't successful. I hadn't had many books/stories published. The dream of making money from my writing was still a dream. I didn't think I wanted to be a writer anymore. And why was I doing this again?

This made me sad and depressed. I won't go into the depression here; that's another story. Suffice to say, I was miserable.

Every morning I'd turn on my computer, read through the last paragraphs of the story I was working on and expect to continue writing as I'd always done.

Instead, I found I couldn't write another word.

Despite persevering for weeks, I grew more morose until I couldn't turn on the computer without weeping.

One day – while I was *not* writing – I found an internet site about, what else, writing. The message was: if you want to give up

writing then do so. Stop procrastinating and driving your family

mad with your moaning/misery. Give up, don't write anymore,

stop.

So, I decided to stop writing. I told myself I was finished with

writing, that I'd never write again.

I took out all my writing folders and found my shredder. I

remember thinking, 'this will finish me off altogether!' but,

strangely, I began to feel better. Why had I kept all these faded

unwanted, unpublished manuscripts, pages stuck together with

now rusty staples? I'd moved house with all this rubbish. It was

way past time it went through the shredder.

So I continued shredding my manuscripts.

Then I came upon one of my short stories I'd written years ago.

Yes, it was unpublished. But I *liked* the story. I didn't want to part

with it. This worn copy was the only one I had. I couldn't shred it.

So I put it to one side and continued.

Published stories – a bare three or four – I couldn't contemplate shredding either. I put them with my short story I wanted to keep, a small 'vanity collection' I might one day show my grandchildren.

Next, I came upon my children's stories. Again, a bare three or four were published. Others were at various stages of completion: complete but still needing work, or still at the beginning/idea stage. I couldn't shred those, so added them to my pile.

I grew confused. Why was I keeping my writing? I'd finished writing, hadn't I?

The story I'd been working on, beckoned. I turned on my computer and began reading, feeling my spirits sink with each paragraph I read. It was a load of crap!

My finger hovered over the delete button, but in the end I couldn't delete something that had taken me almost two years to write.

My confusion – and misery – deepened. What to do? Was I giving up writing, or not?

I didn't know, so I left everything as it was; a messy office full of shredded words and faded sheets of paper spread out like too many ghosts.

Two or three days later, still despondent, I went out to the letterbox – and found a letter from a publisher. Earlier in the year, I had sent them one of my children's picture book manuscripts. I stared at the letter a long time before finding the courage to open it, knowing in my heart it would help me decide on my writing future.

They wanted to publish my book! I recall my tears, the way my hands trembled as I read the letter again and again. I did a little dance up the driveway.

Maybe I *could* write?

What caused my writer's block?

To be honest, I think I'd allowed my dismay and disappointment at my 'unsuccessful' writing career to rule my feelings, to overwhelm me, to block my creativity.

Inner Belief

Even writing this now reminds me of how swamped I'd allowed myself to become.

I had to find courage and inner belief in myself to resume my writing career.

Negativity is a block. We have to replace negativity with positive, encouraging thoughts. Every positive, encouraging thought is a step up, a literal and figurative push along our writing path.

We need to *believe* in ourselves.

The Measure of Success

Over the years, I've learnt that success is not only measured by publishing success, or monetary success, or even fame.

What means the most now is when someone tells me they loved one of my books or they enjoyed reading one of my short stories. When I hear a grandchild wants one of my children's picture books read to them every night, it brings tears to my eyes. There's nothing to top the feeling you've made someone happy or that you've brought laughter into a child's life.

I'll add here the achievement of having written something *you* enjoy, something that has made you smile, or even cry, is a success, too.

To Re-Cap What We Covered in Chapter Three

* Inspiration

Inspiration is everywhere; in our familiar surroundings, our work/home life, our travels or at our local café.

* The Power of Words

Make every word count. There are millions of words; you will never run out.

* Keywords

Use keywords to gather your thoughts or ideas for a story.

* Write at Your Own Pace

Don't be concerned at what others are doing, or how fast they write; everyone writes at their own pace.

* Productivity

Some days are more productive than others.

* Creative Time

Work out your most creative time. Don't waste it on mundane tasks.

* Tricks of the Trade and Safety Nets for Your Ideas

Take a writing break.

End each writing session in the middle of a paragraph so you can continue next day without hesitation.

* Writer's Block

My story

* Inner Belief

Every positive, encouraging thought is a step up, a literal and figurative push along your writing path.

* The Measure of Success

Success is measured by many things.

4 FIRST EDITING SESSION AND TIME MANAGEMENT

Chapter Four has your first editing session. There are sections on time management, how to cope with negativity, and ways to break your writing into manageable amounts.

Plus Exercise Six.

Ideas from Our Surroundings

Never underestimate the power of imagination.

We use our imagination to write our stories, and can add authenticity by experiencing for ourselves the topic we're writing about – if possible.

By this I mean if you want to know the taste and texture of mushrooms eat a few. If you want to know whether sand squeaks underfoot walk barefoot on a beach.

Exercise Six

- Write a short description of a person walking along the beach or through a park/farmland/forest.

- Again, if it helps, find a photograph of the chosen locale.

- Visit one of these locations if possible. There's nothing like the real thing to clear your mind and make it work.

- Take full note of your surroundings and use all your senses. What shape is the mountain? Is the bark of the huge old oak tree rough or smooth? Does snow melt on your tongue? What is the consistency of mud? Is the ocean salty?

- Always incorporate the five senses in your stories. And don't forget your sixth sense!

Find Your Way of Writing

- Record your observations on your phone and transcribe them later, or take a notebook with you.

- Remember, there are no rules in writing. No one is watching over your shoulder and wagging a finger at you saying you're not doing it the right way. There's no 'right' way to write, just different ways. Find *your* way. Use *everything* to your advantage, including time and place.

- Don't stifle your writing with conformity; welcome poetry and lyricism into your work. Use your observations of life, and your knowledge of human character.

- Bypass overblown descriptions: dark and stormy night, dappled light, vigorous growth, bushy glen, autumn leaves, wind-whipped tide, sparkling waters/sea, the crash of thunder, etc.

- Find your own descriptions and your own way of writing.

- Once again, try your hand at writing your own piece before you read my example.

- It's not a competition. We all view the world differently.

- Keep enthusiasm uppermost in your mind.

Example:

The sea was angry today, as angry as I felt. It surged against the shoreline, bent on gouging out a new path for its wild waves to rule. I leapt out of the way of the great curving hand of the surge before it caught me in its foamy grip.

I hurried on, clambering over swathes of smelly seaweed and flotsam that had accumulated along the beach in unbroken lines. Silver splashes of broken shells glinted from the rubble, inviting me to pick them up, to wonder at what form they had once taken.

At the mouth of the river I paused, watching the river race and run, and beat at a huge tree that lay at loggerheads with the swollen tide.

My breath came faster at the sight, and tears stung. I told myself it was the wind. But the ugliness of the previous night taunted me. I saw him dashing for his car, his shape and form unrecognizable in the rain and hazy streetlight. I heard the sound of the motor revving into life then being swallowed up by the wildness as he drove away.

At last I turned to retrace my steps. A woman walked toward me, her red scarf flapping out behind her like a ripped sail. Her small dog barked over the roar of the waves.

"Quite a storm last night," she yelled as our paths crossed. Her dog yipped and bounced around her in full agreement.

"Yes!" I yelled back, pretending to forge my way up and over a large clump of seaweed. I waved and hurried on my way, not in the mood for weather talk, for raking over the debris of last night's storm.

Editing

Before we move on, let's do a short editing session – the first.

Editing isn't as difficult as you might think. Never be afraid to edit your work. It's yours to change.

Read the following sentence:

'I had to leap out of the way of the surge as it flung out a great curving hand as if to catch me in its foamy grip.'

This was my original sentence in the piece above. When I re-read the sentence I decided I didn't like it, that I could do better.

I changed it to:

'I leapt out of the way of the great curving hand of the surge before it caught me in its foamy grip.'

What do you think of the changed sentence? Does it read better?

Add more to the scene as a whole? I feel it adds a splash of danger and reflects the protagonist's inner musings. She isn't fully focused on her immediate surroundings, she's thinking about the previous evening, her own emotional storm.

This is how you can use setting as a character, and to reflect your character's thoughts and inner emotions.

Let's look at the following sentence:

'Silver splashes of broken shells glinted from the rubble, inviting me to pick them up, to wonder at what form they had once taken.'

This sentence also reflects how the protagonist feels.

The shells are 'broken' and lying in the rubble; the protagonist's relationship is 'broken'. She imagines the shells are inviting her to 'wonder at what form they had once taken' when they were whole, as she was before the 'debris of last night's storm'.

Look at the word 'glinted'. Would sparkled, flashed, winked, shone, spangled or twinkled worked better? Why not? To me they're not strong enough, which is why I used 'glinted'.

Always take the time, when editing, to find the right word, the word that describes exactly what you mean. Don't stop writing to spend minutes searching for the word; underline it and come back to it at the editing stage.

I wish I'd followed that advice in the early days of writing, instead of allowing word searches to take me right out of my story.

Write first; edit later.

Time Management for Writing

Mountains and Molehills

Don't make mountains out of molehills or put obstacles in your path. Try to get rid of obstacles and negativity.

Writing takes time, especially writing a book. It's easy to shrug and say, 'I haven't time to write a book because I work full-time'. Or, 'I have a family to care for', 'my weekends are full' or 'I'm waiting until I retire then I'll have the time to write'.

There's always spare time if we stop and think. I've worked full-time and still found time to write. Even though I prefer to write in the morning I had to retrain myself and convince myself I could write at night.

Every night after dinner I'd sit at my computer and write, no matter how tired I was. In the beginning it was hard but after a while I looked forward to my nightly writing sessions. I could see I was getting somewhere; my word bank was building, my chapters were forming. Another bonus was that I began to enjoy my characters and couldn't wait to see what adventures I could lead them into and through each night.

By following this one principle, and sticking at it, I completed my novel.

That's the way I've written this book. By building each chapter from page one. By recording ideas, keywords and headings when I thought of them and expanding on them later.

Always record ideas as you think of them. Don't leave it and think you'll remember them. You won't, and this can be frustrating, as I've learned to my cost.

If you set yourself a goal of writing every day, then find you can't achieve this goal, you're setting yourself up to fail. It's better to write whenever you can find the time, even if it's half an hour here, and an hour or two there. The main thing is to keep at it, even if you're forced to hide in the bathroom!

People often ask me how I find the time to write. My answer is you have to be fairly ruthless with your spare time. Don't fill up this time by cleaning the kitchen, or watching television, or mooching through the mall to check out the latest fashions/computer software. Don't waste precious spare time.

If you're determined to write, you *will* find the time, even if your

housework doesn't get done as often. You should see my floors –
maybe not!

It's about *beginning*. Once you've jumped over that hurdle then
you're underway; especially if your goal is to write a novel.

Compare writing a novel to climbing a mountain. You can make
that mountain vast and unconquerable and give up before you
even begin. Or you can imagine it the size of a small hill and plan
your way up those slippery slopes. This might be a zigzag path, but
if you achieve small steps each day – writing as often as you can –
then you'll climb that mountain.

Another analogy I often use is painting the roof. You climb up the
ladder and peer at the roof. It's bigger than you remembered; a
Herculean task. You put away your ladder and paint and
paintbrushes. You'll tackle the roof another day when you're in
the right frame of mind, when there's time or when the weather
is fine.

These obstacles in your path are your convictions the task is beyond you. It will take too much time to complete and you'll never achieve it.

How to Tackle that Roof

Draw a rough diagram of the roof. Block out several sections into manageable lots, areas you could paint in one or two days, or even one or two hours. Work out the day/time you'll begin.

Now your task has moved from insurmountable to achievable. You still have to find time, and naturally your task will be weather permitting. But you've overcome the most obstinate of your obstacles. You'll be working out when you can start and perhaps enthusiasm will strike because you've cut the job down to size.

Visualize the job completed, the roof gleaming with its new coat of paint. Imagine your pleasure and relief when you've achieved your objective.

If you *want* to paint the roof/house, you'll have plenty of spare time whilst painting – hours when your mind will float free. Use this time to 'write'. Take your phone with you and record your thoughts. Never waste a minute.

You can put this principle into use for other household tasks; vacuuming, dusting, washing or cleaning of any kind. Always have your phone or notebook handy to record ideas, keywords and headings or notes for your next chapter.

Powers of Observation

Exercise Seven

- Imagine you're painting a roof/house/garage. It doesn't have to be your own house.
- Picture yourself or your character on the roof, painting.

- Imagine the view. What can you see/hear/smell/touch/taste? What's happening? Are there any wild animals lurking in the woods at the rear of the house? What boats are anchored in the harbor? What are your neighbors doing? Who is that person arriving in the jazzy sports car?

- Let your imagination have free rein. By asking questions, you get answers. Those answers might be the beginning of a short story or a mystery novel.

- The aim of the exercise is to notice what's happening in your neighborhood and surrounding area.

- If you don't fancy the roof, park your car somewhere – your local town/park – and observe your surroundings.

- Or perhaps you'd prefer a café or your local library or even a bus trip.

- Train yourself to be 'nosey'. Writers are inquisitive. Writers – and readers – love to discover what others are doing.

- Try to write at least one to two pages.

- Don't be daunted by these exercises. Think of them as your writing session for the day/week. It's easy to think, 'I can't be bothered doing that one, it's too hard'. Or, 'I'll wait until there's something easier, or something that won't take me long to do'.

- You don't have to make your writing nice, or write about a nice, comfortable day in the life of your protagonist. That can be humdrum. Instead, try imagining an unusual character. Or a mysterious event that has everyone in your street speculating.

- Imagine how things appear during the different seasons, day/night.

Point of View

You don't always have to write about yourself or from your own experiences – your point of view. I've written stories from many viewpoints, and so have other writers.

Why not experiment with writing from the POV of an older or younger person of a different gender? It's not as difficult as you might think. Imagine yourself in your character's skin. What problems do they face? How do they react when faced with their problems? Is it fight or flight?

By standing in your character's shoes, you'll soon find the answers to your questions.

Example:

He arrived in the early morning darkness, briefcase and complaints at the ready which he dropped at my feet the minute the front door closed behind him. Groggy with sleep and resignation I let it wash over me, the same old excuses and emotional blackmail I'd heard a hundred times.

Once, in the early days, I'd have clucked with sympathy and rushed to the kitchen to heat a meal or make him his favorite hot cocoa drink. Not anymore. Now I stood silently waiting for it to end.

He was mid-ramble when he spied the travel folder on the kitchen table. I'd put it there on purpose, telling myself resentfully that he deserved it. His mouth hung open. Talk about a stunned mullet!

"What's this, then?"

Once he'd had the power to make my insides quiver with that sneering tone. Not anymore. I threw off my grogginess, crossed to the table and picked up the folder.

"My travel documents." I stuffed them into the pocket of my dressing-gown; worried he might snatch them and rip them to pieces as he'd once done with my 'Certificate for Competence in English Studies'.

"You! Competent? In English? Studies?" Each had been

delivered with the full complement of scorn. "Get real, Janie."

"I'm going, tomorrow, Barry. And I don't want arguments."

I left him, mouth still open, lips moving like a dying fish, and went back to bed.

How to Plan Your Story

If you're still not sure how to begin, planning is the answer.

Let's use the analogy of the roof in the above exercise. Imagine a ladder leaning against the wall of the house. Each rung represents a section of your story; the first rung the beginning, the last rung the ending and the rungs In between the middle of your story.

- Draw a ladder on your page.

- In the first section write a few words/sentences that could work as the beginning of your story; your character's mood and thoughts.

- In each of the following sections write a list of things he/she might notice from his/her position, and their reaction to these things: trees, animals, boats, cars, neighbors, loud exhaust, lawnmower, the smell of the river, the arrival of a stranger.

- In the last section of the ladder write a few words/sentences for the ending of your story. The way your character might view his/her life now, or what he/she might have learnt through their experience.

Experiment with different endings – a popular trend for mysteries and whodunits. You can ask family or friends to choose the one they like best, or post your examples on-line and ask readers to vote for their favorite ending. Get your readers involved from the beginning.

These 'ladders' are called mind maps and are an excellent way of finding ideas, then expanding on those ideas.

How to Fight Negativity

Don't listen to detractors. There are always those who discourage.

They'll tell you writing is difficult, that you need an English degree,

or experience in journalism or teaching. Perhaps they'll smugly

point out you're entering a competitive field, especially if you

want to be a published author.

There's always someone prepared to put you off; ignore them.

To Re-Cap What We Covered in Chapter Four

* Ideas from Our Surroundings

Visit the park/beach/forest or any other area you want to write about and note your surroundings.

* Your Way of Writing

Find the way of writing that suits you.

* Editing

Your first editing session.

*Time Management for Writing

Mountains and Molehills.

Don't put obstacles in your path.

* How to Tackle that Roof

Use the roof analogy to break your writing into manageable lots.

* Powers of Observation

Write a piece describing events in your neighborhood, using your

powers of observation.

* Point Of View

You don't always have to write about yourself or from your own experiences – your POV.

* How to Plan Your Story

Plan your story using mind maps as prompts.

*How to Fight Negativity

Don't listen to detractors; put your energies into self-belief.

5 GENERAL AND SPECIFIC SENTENCES

Who, What, When, Where, Why?

Chapter Five looks at how to use general, then specific, sentences to form your first sentence/paragraph. There are examples of how to build a character profile, and how not to turn your hero into a cliché.

General and Specific Sentences

Who, what, when, where and why

A man arrived that afternoon.

He rode into town that hot afternoon.

The new sheriff rode into town when the heat of the afternoon was at its worst.

Sheriff Roan McDermott rode into town when the heat of the afternoon had dragged most citizens to the point of stupor.

Sheriff Roan McDermott rode into town when the heat of the afternoon had dragged most of Doubtful Valley's citizens to the point of stupor.

Who, What, When and Where

The sentence paints a picture, introduces the hero, and answers the important questions; who, what, when, and where.

Always begin your stories by introducing your main protagonist.

The next sentence 'he rode into town that hot afternoon',

presents a picture of the hero riding into town. You can see the dust kicking up behind him as he rides along, the sheen of perspiration on his face.

The story is a Western – your genre.

The protagonist needs a strong name, not the name of an outlaw. Then again, the hero might be a reformed outlaw? What is his history? You want your readers keen to know everything – *you* need to know everything.

So the questions, 'who,' 'what,' and 'when' have been answered.

Now, we deepen the introduction to show 'where' the action will take place, the setting – the town of Doubtful Valley.

Always be aware that setting is a 'character' and plays a vital role in your stories.

Note the last part of the sentence; 'when the heat had dragged most of Doubtful Valley's citizens to the point of stupor'.

The sentence introduces the whole town; Doubtful Valley. We're told most of the citizens are at 'the point of stupor'. This is done by personifying the word heat. The citizens are lying around all but dead from the heat, from *defeat*. We don't need to be told something has happened in the town to 'drag' the people down; it's not just the heat.

Always think how words work to paint pictures, to introduce characters and human emotion.

By beginning with general sentences then graduating to specific sentences you'll soon build that all important first paragraph – your first *scene*.

Why

The why is always implied in the first sentence; *why* is Sheriff Roan McDermott in Doubtful Valley?

By asking other questions, we find the answer. How long is he going to stay? Is he after someone? What business has he in the town? Why has he arrived today of all days?

Character Profile

Continue to develop your character profile by asking questions: age, height, weight, birth date, family, marital state, past careers/jobs, religion, friends – where you often find secondary characters. Save in a separate file under the hero's name. You might use all the information, or not. Either way, you'll grow to know your hero in more depth.

Some writers can't begin their stories unless they have full knowledge of their protagonist from the outset. If that's what you prefer, then do it. If you prefer to get to know your hero as you progress through your story, that's also fine.

As I mentioned before there are no set rules, only a way that suits you. Both ways are acceptable, and most writers probably use both.

I always love it when a character does something that makes me wonder why they've behaved in that way. When I wonder *why*, I always find the answer. It's one of the exciting discoveries in writing *character*.

How Not to Turn Your Hero into a Cliché

Don't turn your hero into a cliché by writing a long paragraph describing him as tall dark and handsome with a sunburned face and wearing a battered Stetson low on his brow. This turns your hero into a cliché, and is likely to turn your readers away as they mutter, 'I've read this before/seen the film/bought the tee-shirt'. You don't want them tossing your book aside after reading the first sentence.

Describe your protagonist through the eyes of another character –

always the best way in my opinion.

You might recall the examples in Chapter One, how the characters were shown through the eyes of another.

The Second Sentence

The second sentence builds the same way as the first, beginning with a general sentence and graduating to a more specific sentence.

I saw him from our verandah.

I saw him from our verandah where I'd gone after lunch.

I saw him from our verandah – where I'd gone after lunch to fight for a breath of air.

I saw him from our verandah – where I'd gone after lunch to fight for a breath of air – and thought how splendid he looked.

I saw him from our verandah – where I'd gone after lunch to fight for a breath of air – and thought how splendid he looked wearing the dust and the heat.

I saw him from our verandah – where I'd gone after lunch to fight for a breath of air – and thought how splendid he looked wearing the dust and the heat like armor.

Our Second Character

Here is our second character, the heroine? The gender is not revealed, yet we sense the character is a woman. Study the words describing the character. 'Our verandah' sounds possessive in a feminine way. I see her hugging the verandah post, transfixed by the hero.

Always imagine how and where your characters are positioned.

The word 'splendid' to describe the hero is more likely the way a woman describes a man.

'Where I'd gone after lunch to fight for a breath of air' lets the reader know the heroine has spirit and determination that she's prepared to fight despite 'everything'. She is literally seeking air where there's none. Figuratively, she's 'seeing what might be done'.

The sentence works to deepen the atmosphere of oppression – the heat and the dust, the 'oppressive air'.

Her last thoughts present a picture of the hero. He is 'splendid'. He wears the dust and heat 'like armor'. Again, 'dust' and 'heat' are personified. The hero is a man who wears 'armor'; against the world, everyone, the heroine?

Look again at the words, splendid, dust, heat, and armor. The hero sounds battle-hardened, or about to go into battle. There's the impression he doesn't notice the heat or the dust. But he'll be aware of the 'oppressive air' hanging over the town and the townsfolk.

The reader *knows* there's going to be fireworks, and soon.

Show, Don't Tell

By introducing your characters in this way, by placing them in a setting where they're 'in their element' you paint a picture of them in a few words. You are *showing* them to your readers, not *telling* your readers what to think of them.

Your readers need to make up their own minds about your characters, not be told the hero is one tough man, hardened and embittered by life. Or that the heroine is spirited and prepared to fight for her principles. They need to understand this through the character's actions/thoughts.

Who's Point of View?

The first sentence is from the heroine's POV. It's the heroine's voice we hear, or in this case, her thoughts. We're seeing the hero ride into Doubtful Valley through her eyes. Thoughts are internal dialogue.

POV can be confusing. It's wise to stay in one person's POV to avoid confusing the reader.

Be sure of POV.

It's perfectly acceptable to write from several viewpoints throughout your story. Begin the next chapter from the hero's POV with him settling into the town, reflecting on why he's here and considering the heroine – because he'll have noticed her.

How to Introduce Tension

Before we move away from the story, let's examine another sentence or two which takes the scene to the next level, and introduces tension. We'll use the same strategy of beginning with a general sentence then moving on to more specific sentences.

Something went past my face then.

Something went past my face then and it wasn't the longed-for breeze I'd been seeking.

It was all I could do to keep my grip on the verandah railing.

It was all I could do to keep my grip on the verandah railing as I wondered who he was.

It was all I could do to keep my grip on the verandah railing as I wondered who this man was, what his coming here into my world meant.

This introduces tension, the first questions. The heroine sounds protective of her world 'our verandah' and 'my world'. The hero's arrival shakes the heroine's world – 'It was all I could do to keep my grip on the verandah railing'.

By building one sentence on top of the other in this fashion, you expand the story and invite your reader to read on and find out what happens.

The next sentence takes that process further.

I thought he'd glance my way.

I thought he'd glance my way; indeed, my feminine vanity demanded he should.

I thought he'd glance my way; indeed, my feminine vanity – and another female curiosity I hardly knew – demanded he should.

When he didn't, a strange rage made me want to run out into that hot afternoon.

When he didn't, a strange rage made me want to run out into that hot afternoon and demand to know his business.

How dare he ride past in that manner!

How dare he ride past in that manner as if I was nothing!

How dare he ride past in that manner as if I was nothing, as if the whole town was nothing but more red dust to shake from his dusty boots!

Examine each sentence, and the way they build in sequence. Is a picture forming in your mind of both hero and heroine, of the action that will happen later in the story?

The hero rides past, ignoring the heroine, 'throwing down the gauntlet'. The heroine hasn't the courage yet to pick up that gauntlet, but the reader knows she will.

Exercise Eight

- Change these sentences around to present a different picture of both hero and heroine.

- Write the scene from the hero's POV. Incorporate his first impressions of the town, the heroine and the townsfolk.

- Allow yourself privy to your protagonist's thoughts. Judge the town, the townsfolk and the heroine through his eyes.

- Remember, these are my words. You need to write *your* words, in *your* way.

- If you don't know the Western genre, don't let that faze you. Set yourself a challenge and try the exercise. You might be surprised at what you write.

- Start with a small township, or a single house, or the desert itself. Imagine the people and their adventures.

- Don't forget photographs, keywords and mind maps.

- Research the Western genre, the desert or that period of history.

- Any of these points will get you started.

Which Characters to Choose

How do we choose the right characters? Which character should we introduce first?

It's a decision writer's face, even with planning. They may have written – and labored over – that first chapter, or even several chapters, then realize they've started the story in the wrong place, and with the wrong character.

If this happens to you, don't panic and discard those first chapters. Keep them. Recognize you have a better understanding of your characters and their motivations.

Nothing is ever wasted. You might have needed to write that first chapter to understand your characters and their motivations. Know that you're now well into your writer zone, and comfortable with the way the story will develop.

This happened with one of my novels. I struggled with the first chapter, and wondered why I was struggling. No matter what I wrote, it wasn't right. When my editor pointed out that although my character was an important character, she wasn't the protagonist. As soon as she said this, I realized it was the truth. I began again with my protagonist, and the story flowed from there.

Our Writer's Soul

In every piece of writing a part of the writer is revealed, our writer's soul, if you will. It doesn't matter if we write fiction or non-fiction; a part of who we are is unconsciously revealed.

The realization can be a shock at first. But that's what being a writer means; to write with honesty. It makes our stories moving and more intense. We are sharing our own/our character's innermost emotions with our reader.

Imagine diving deep into the ocean where the clarity, intensity and power of the blue takes your breath away. You are one with that mighty entity as it sweeps around you, below you and above you, seemingly into eternity. At that moment, in that exquisite wrap of water, anything is possible.

We need to bring that same intensity to our stories.

It's natural to hold back and think, 'I won't write that because it's too personal'.

We need to let go of this final barrier, to float with freedom and without inhibition.

In class, I was aware this was one of the main reasons students didn't want to read their work out loud. Sometimes there were tears as the writer had written something personal. When they found the courage to share – what reward for the rest of us.

Picture your favorite books, those that hold a special place in your heart and resonate long after you've finished reading them. Chances are you've read a writer who has captured the emotional depth of their character, moved you to tears or laughter or both, and made you *care* what happened to their characters.

These are the writers we aspire to emulate.

Don't hold back in your writing. Dive into those depths. You'll find more satisfaction than you can imagine and your readers will applaud your efforts.

To Re-Cap What We Covered in Chapter Five

* General and Specific

How to use specific sentences, not general sentences, to build your stories.

* The First Sentence

How to introduce your protagonist and answer the important questions; who, what, when, where and why.

* How to Build a Character Profile

Build a character profile by asking questions about your

protagonist.

* How Not to Turn Your Hero into a Cliché

Don't turn your hero into a cliché.

* The Second Sentence

How the first sentence builds into the second sentence.

* Your Second Character

How to introduce your second character.

* Show, Don't Tell

Don't *tell* the reader how your character is feeling. *Show* your

character's emotions through action and let the reader decide for

themselves.

* Who's Point of View

Be clear on POV.

* Introducing Tension

How to introduce tension into your stories.

* Which Characters to Choose

How do we choose the right characters? Which character should

we introduce first?

* Our Writer's Soul

We can't help but reveal a part of ourselves in our writing.

6 A SHORT STORY

Writing The Short Story

In Chapter Six there's my short story, *The Return,* for you to read.

At last, I hear you say!

You might think short stories are easy to write because they're short, but they are difficult to get just right. It takes practice – that word again – but don't give up after the first few attempts. Keep writing; and read lots of short stories to see how other writers achieve the elements needed for a good short story.

I've written many short stories over the years, and there's nothing more satisfying than seeing your protagonists complete the journey you've set for them.

The Protagonist's Journey

First you need an opening for your story where you introduce your protagonist and infer a problem that needs sorting out. Your protagonist embarks on their journey of trying to sort out this problem – the middle of your story – which takes up the larger part of the story.

The ending resolves the problem. You don't always have to write a happy ending but it does need to be satisfying and not leave problems unresolved or questions unanswered; to do so risks annoying your reader and you want them to finish your story and look forward to your next one.

Below is my short story, *The Return, New Zealand Woman's Weekly* 1994.

Read it through first in one sitting then we'll examine each section in Chapter Seven.

The Return

The concrete was grey and unfriendly beneath my feet, an impassive spectator of my return. People brushed by me, but I didn't look at them. I wasn't yet ready to exchange smiles and nods of recognition, or talk to old friends.

"You can't go back," Mum had said. "Nothing stays the same. People change. You make new friends." Perhaps she was right, but I had to find out for myself.

I walked slowly along the street, past the sports shop, the bank and the bakery. I stopped in front of the gift shop. Once I'd bought a dainty glass cat from the silver-haired lady who owned the shop. As elegant and fragile as the gifts she sold, she would have understood my reasons for coming back. But she'd gone years ago.

Fighting back tears, I moved on. There was the bookshop where Matty had won ten dollars on an Instant Kiwi ticket.

"We've won!" he had laughed. "Come on, I'll buy you the biggest ice-cream there is." And we had run along to the new ice-cream parlor and bought huge green ice-creams with lumps of red jelly in the middle.

I reached the center of the town and automatically turned down the little side road that led to the river. It was still the same, still rushing past in a muddy green flow with the overhanging trees just clearing the swirling surface. Ducks were huddled in the long grass out of the wind.

I looked across at the bush. Soon it would be spring and the kowhai would paint the riverbank in gold.

I twisted the gold wedding ring on my finger.

"Marry me, Sally," Matty had said, his young face earnest. "It'll be an adventure. Just you and me, Sal."

His blue eyes had been full of excitement as he had planned our future. "We'll go to Australia, like our great great-grandparents did. Oh, I know there's no gold rush." His expression had been sheepish.

Then he had grinned and caught my hand. "We'll go digging for opals instead." And he had laughed a spontaneous sound of joy that enthralled all who heard it.

"But Sally, you're only sixteen," Mum had protested. "What about school?" She had turned to Dad. "You tell her, David. She can't possibly get married."

Dad had shrugged and given a lop-sided grin. "I know she's young, dear. But ...I already think of Matty as our son."

There had been no more protests. Mum liked Matty as much as Dad did. As we had been on the verge of shifting, that had clinched the matter.

Mary had practically lived at our house ever since we had moved there, just after my fourth birthday. Matty had been nine. I hadn't taken much notice of him then. He and my older brother, Brett, were always off fishing somewhere and didn't want a kid like me tagging along. Even when his parents had shifted down country, Matty had stayed on with us, boarding with us...

I went back to the main street. The lights were on in the dairy across the road. The usual crowd of teenagers hung around the entrance. Some were draped over the wrought iron staircase that led to rooms above the shop next door.

I was going to walk on, pretend I hadn't seen them. But I made myself stop and look across at each person. Kylie, Heather, Alison, Jackie, Glennis and two others I didn't know. Most of the old gang. My school friends.

They'd seen me. I lifted one hand in a half-wave and tried to smile. A couple of them responded in kind, while the others shuffled about, not looking at me. I hadn't answered any of their letters. The street was between us. Should I go over?

A car roared past, its exhaust shattering the moment.

"What're ya doing later?" a voice, almost as loud as the exhaust, yelled across at the girls.

As one, they turned and yelled back. Everything from, "Nothing!" to "Get lost!"

I moved on in the wake of the exhaust fumes. I didn't want to talk to any of them anyway. They all seemed so young. Scatty teenagers.

I could hardly believe that 18 months ago we had been at school together. It seemed a million years ago.

I reached the end of the street and looked up at the clock. Nearly five o'clock. It got dark early in winter. I watched the last of the shoppers hurrying home and was thankful I didn't know any of them.

Another car swung past. I waited until it had gone, then

crossed the street.

The lights in the fish and chip shop glared and the wire mesh door banged loudly as someone came out. Two youths sauntered past, laughing and joking, and already tearing at the paper around their fish and chips. I smelt hot chips and salt.

It was time to go. Matty would be getting hungry. I'd walk back along this side of the street. Do the loop. For old time's sake. Mum was waiting for me back at the car.

I stopped to look in the jeweler's window. The collection of rings gleamed yellow, blue, gold and silver beneath the lights.

"We'll have an engagement ring made from the first stone we find," Matty had said. But Matty had been killed on his way out to his first dig. "I'll go first, Sal," he had insisted. "Make sure it's safe."

I scrubbed at my face. Mum was right. It had been a mistake to come back. I was glad of the semi-darkness as I hurried toward the car.

I'd forgotten about the dairy and the people who were still clustered round the entrance. They were the last people in the world I wanted to see now.

"Hi, Sally." It was Kylie, flicking back her long red hair, almost blocking my way. Kylie had been my best friend.

"Hi," she said again, quieter now. I was conscious of voices fading, shuffling feet and a few self-conscious coughs.

'Hi, Sally," someone else said. But I didn't look. There was silence. They didn't know what to say any more than I did.

"Sally! There you are." It was Mum, hurrying along the street. She was pushing Matty's pram. My cheeks burned. I hadn't told anyone about Matty. I had refused to let Mum and Dad put a birth notice in the paper. Matty was nearly three months old.

Having children so soon hadn't exactly been on our agenda. But Matty had taken the news in his usual enthusiastic way. And that golden laughter had rung out.

"Another pair of hands to help with the digging," he had joked.

The sight of my mother pushing a pram had an electrifying effect on the group of girls. They straightened up. Hair was patted, clothes were discretely tugged at and chewing gun disappeared.

I went up to Mum and smiled down at my son. They followed, crowding round the pram, greeting Mum, and then all trying to talk at once.

"Sally! A baby...?" "I didn't know..." "Why didn't you say...?" "Let me see..."

"Can I see...?" "Oh, Sally..."

"Isn't he adorable?" Mum cooed down at Matty.

This seemed to be the cue to unleash a series of similar sounds from each of the girls.

"How old is he, Sally?"

"Oh, he's gorgeous, Sally."

"What big blue eyes!"

In the usual baby talk, reserved for tiny babies, there was admiration, wonder and even a shade of envy. The previous awkwardness had gone. Even the two girls I hadn't met were as close to the pram as they could get.

I bent down and lifted Matty from the pram. Mum made anxious noises about the cold, even though Matty had his woolly hat on. I held him up for the girls to see. They crowded eagerly round.

"Oh, Sally." Kylie put her arm around me. "Why didn't you write?"

Her eyes sparkled with tears. She put her red head against mine and laid a finger on Matty's warm cheek.

I couldn't speak. I heard someone blow her nose. Then hands reached out to gently touch Matty's tiny feet and his little fists.

I swallowed hard. They had lost a friend, too. In a way they had lost two friends.

"Would you like...to hold Matty?" I asked Kylie. My mouth and jaw were stiff but I managed to get the words out.

"Could I?" Kylie breathed. Everyone seemed to hold their breath as Kylie reached for Matty. He wriggled a bit and made a funny little noise. Everyone laughed. Then Kylie handed him back to me and I tucked him into his pram.

"Are you coming up again soon?" Kylie fell into step beside me. The others trailed along behind, talking to Mum.

"I don't know." I looked at her face and realized how much I had missed her friendship. For a moment there was silence then we were hugging each other fiercely.

"I'll write," I promised and got into the car. We held hands, bridging the car window and the months of silence. As Mum started the car and we pulled away from the curb, I let go Kylie's hand and waved.

In a way, Mum had been right. Nothing stayed the same. And you did make new friends. But old friends were always there.

As I looked back along the street, Matty made another one of his funny little noises and, in the sound, I thought I heard the echo of his father's laughter.

The End

To Re-Cap What We Covered in Chapter Six

* Writing The Short Story

To write a short story takes practice. Read other short stories to see how other writers achieve the elements needed for a good short story.

* The Protagonist's Journey

The opening introduces the protagonist and infers a problem that needs sorting out. The protagonist embarks on their journey of trying to sort out this problem – the middle of your story – which takes up the larger part of the story.

The ending resolves the problem. You don't always have to write a happy ending but it does need to be satisfying and not leave problems unresolved or questions unanswered; to do so risks annoying your reader and you want them to finish your story and look forward to your next one.

* My Short Story: *The Return*

7 HOW TO CONSTRUCT A SHORT STORY

In Chapter Seven I'll take you through the steps of constructing a short story. There are many ways of beginning your stories, of introducing your protagonist/s; mine is one example.

As I've explained before, with each piece of writing there is a beginning, middle and an end. That might sound difficult to achieve, but with *practice*, you can soon learn the intricacies of this writing procedure.

In my early days of writing I didn't know these techniques. When I began the structured writing lessons I learnt the principles of writing and how to put them into practice. Until then I'd been forging ahead on my own with no real idea of what I was doing.

We can all learn technique.

Step One: The Beginning

The beginning introduces the protagonist, poses the problem and shows how the protagonist intends to approach/tackle their problem. Always begin with the protagonist. Think of each sentence as a step forward in the protagonist's journey.

Sally's problem is shown by the sentence, "You can't go back," Mum had said. "Nothing stays the same. People change. You make new friends."

"Perhaps she was right. But I had to find out for myself," shows how Sally will approach/tackle her problem.

The reader understands Sally's desire to search out the truth for herself and joins her on her journey.

Sally wants to be alone on her nostalgic trip down memory lane. "I wasn't yet ready to exchange smiles and nods of recognition, or talk to old friends."

The personification of the concrete as 'unfriendly' and 'an impassive spectator' helps underline Sally's feeling of aloneness. There won't be any help from her surroundings. They haven't changed, but she has.

Her recollection of the silver-haired lady is another insight into Sally's state of mind. She 'fights back tears'. Is she remembering only the lady or someone else as well?

At the bookshop, the reader learns of Sally's husband, Matty, and how they had once bought 'huge green ice-creams with lumps of red jelly in the middle'. Life was once carefree and happy, even child-like; but not now.

When Sally reaches the center of town, she automatically turns down the little side road that leads to the river, suggesting she's done this countless times, that here she might find answers and explanations.

What she finds is the river, still the same, still rushing past in a muddy green flow. Life goes on impassively. The seasons still 'turn' regardless of what happens in our lives – 'Soon it would be spring and the kowhai would paint the riverbank in gold'.

As Sally twists her gold wedding ring, the reader suspects what's happened but has yet to have their suspicions confirmed.

In the following paragraphs, and the last of the beginning section, through what is called a flashback, the reader learns Matty and Sally's history. How they married early and went on an adventure, how all things were possible when they were young and full of life – the 'spring' of their lives.

Step Two: The Middle Section: Peaks and Troughs, Gray Spots

The middle section deepens the story and presents more problems for the protagonist. These problems are resolved *at the time*, although the main problem remains unresolved.

Sally goes back to the main street, back to reality, and her first confrontation. 'The usual crowd of teenagers hung around the entrance.'

Confrontations are called 'gray spots' or 'peaks' in a story. The protagonist faces a challenge and *must* act to resolve the problem.

Sally's confrontation is with her old school friends. She is at a cross-road in her journey. 'I was going to walk on, pretend I hadn't seen them. But I made myself stop and look across at each person.' This reveals Sally's courage; despite everything that's happened, she finds the courage to face things.

But the street is between them, the line in the sand that no one dare cross. Sally lifts one hand in a half-wave and tries to smile. She is half-way to solving her major problem. She wonders, 'Should I go over?' But a car roars past, 'shattering the moment', resolving the confrontation and dipping the story into a trough.

Sally's major problem remains unresolved as she moves on in the wake of the exhaust fumes, suggesting the confrontation had left a nasty taste in her mouth.

She makes excuses for her behavior – 'I didn't want to talk to them anyway'. She thinks how young they are – scatty teenagers. Her time with them seems like a million years ago, another lifetime.

Sally's still not ready to talk to old friends, to confront her old life. When she reaches the end of the street she realizes it's time to go. It's time to end her nostalgic walk and return to the immediacy of her life now – caring for her baby son. 'Matty would be getting hungry.'

'I'd walk back along this side of the street. Do the loop. For old time's sake.'

Sally will complete the challenge she has set herself; come full circle.

It's when she stops at the jewelry shop that the reader learns of her husband's death. The rings gleam yellow, blue, gold and silver like the engagement ring Matty wanted to give her.

The end of the middle section occurs when Sally scrubs at her face. She reaches the conclusion that, 'Mum was right. It had been a mistake to come back'. She hurries along the street, away from the rings, away from her memories, away from her 'mistake'.

Step Three: The Ending

The ending begins with the final confrontation. The protagonist must face this challenge and either win or lose. It's a transition from the middle section and the start of the end section, but not *right* at the end.

Following this moment – sometimes called the 'black moment' or 'climax' of the story – there's no more conflict, only resolution. All problems are resolved. There must be no questions left; you don't want your readers thinking 'but what happened to so and so?'

The ending begins with the sentence, 'I'd forgotten about the dairy and the people who were still clustered around the entrance'.

Sally approaches her final challenge. How will she react? Your characters always need to *act in character*. Sally is still only young, even though she feels years older in experience than the other 'scatty teenagers'.

The final challenge is shown by aggressive action. Sometimes there's a physical fight. The protagonist *must* win that fight.

Here it's provided by Kylie. 'It was Kylie, flicking back her long red hair, almost blocking my way.' Kylie is challenging Sally, physically and mentally. Sally still doesn't know how to sort out her problem. 'They didn't know what to say anymore than I did.'

Sally *must* act for there to be an outcome to the story.

This happens when Sally's mother arrives with baby Matty. 'The sight of my mother pushing a pram had an electrifying effect on the group of girls.' The baby's innocence is the catalyst to break the deadlock, the silent confrontation between Sally and her school friends.

They literally grow up in that instant. They follow Sally – grown-up Sally who is now a mother – crowding round the pram, greeting Sally's mother and all trying to talk at once, trying to be grown-up.

At last Sally acts. She picks up her baby son and holds him up for the girls to see. He is her pride and joy, Matty's son, her life now.

Animosity and confrontation turns to 'admiration, wonder and even a shade of envy'. The final confrontation is resolved.

Kylie asks why Sally didn't write. 'She put her red head against mine and laid a finger on Matty's warm cheek.' Sally realizes for the first time her loss is not hers alone. 'They had lost a friend, too. In a way they had lost two friends.'

She offers the 'olive branch' by letting Kylie hold her son. Kylie

puts her arm around Sally; friendship is rekindled and restored.

The Resolution

The resolution is when the last explanations occur. It happens

after the climax or final confrontation.

The two girls fall into step. They are now in-step or in tune with

each other again.

'For a moment there was silence, then we were hugging each

other fiercely.' They hold hands, 'bridging the car window and the

months of silence'. They've crossed over to a newer, deeper

friendship.

Sally's last words are a promise to keep their friendship alive. 'I'll write.'

She has found out for herself that 'old friends are always there'.

The Final Sentence

The story could have ended with the above sentence, but if you can add something more that gives the story a final lift, then do this in the final sentence.

I often return to something mentioned in the earlier part of the story, in this case Matty's 'golden laughter'.

'Matty made another one of his funny little noises and, in the sound, I thought I heard the echo of his father's laughter.' This suggests Matty (Sally's husband) has given his 'seal of approval' to how Sally has handled her experience, to the whole of the event. The memory of Matty will live on in Sally's mind.

Themes

The theme is what the story is about: love, happiness, friendship, family conflict, envy, malice, honor, or the need for independence. There might be several themes. What themes are presented in *The Return*?

Plot

Plot is what *happens* in the story. Sally goes back to her hometown. She takes a walk down memory lane. She meets her old school friends.

Questions

You might need to read the story several times before you gain a deeper understanding of how each section works, how each section transitions to the next.

Not every short story follows this formulaic pattern. Literary stories ignore rules and restrictions and flow from the writer's 'streams of consciousness'.

Did I start with the ideas/plans for each section before I began writing the story? No. If I had to do that much planning I doubt I'd ever write.

I often begin my short stories with the first sentence, or an idea, and then write from the sentence or idea until the story is finished. It's the way I write. I prefer to start writing and see where 'the journey of the pen' takes me.

Only when I begin analyzing each story do I discover how the sections have worked, how the story progresses from one section to the next. The editing process is when I change things and add those extra dimensions that lift the story or give explanation. The beginning and the end need the most work, especially the final sentence. It's those final touches that make your story.

Exercise Nine

- Why not try your hand at writing a short story?
- Visit a favorite place and study your surroundings. This is what I did for my story *The Return*. I drove to the small town near where I lived at the time, an area I was familiar with, and sat in the car studying my surroundings. My intent or idea was to write a story from a teenager's POV. I was able to use my observations of the river, the trees, the township and townsfolk to add authenticity to my story.
- Use keywords, mind maps and sentences to get you started.
- Build a character profile of your protagonist.
- Imagine the troubles they might face.

- Decide how your protagonist might tackle/solve their problems.

- Write a beginning, middle and an end, with peaks and troughs throughout your story.

- When you finish your story go back and add a final sentence to give your story a lift.

To Re-Cap What We Covered in Chapter Seven

* How to Construct a Short Story

* The Beginning, Middle and End

* Beginnings

Beginnings introduce the protagonist, state their problem and show how the protagonist will approach/tackle their problem.

* The Middle Section

The middle section deepens the story and presents problems for the protagonist to solve.

* The Ending

The ending resolves the problem.

* The Resolution

The resolution is where the last of the explanations occur. It happens *after* the final confrontation. There must be no questions left.

* The Final Sentence

Search for something mentioned in the beginning of the story and use it at the end to give the story a lift.

* Theme

Theme is what the story is about.

* Plot

Plot is what happens in the story.

* Questions

Questions about the structure of short stories.

8 NOVELS

In Chapter Eight we examine the opening chapter of a novel; how to introduce our protagonist, present their problem and show the manner in which they plan to solve the problem.

The Opening Chapter of My Novel *Progressions*

Zumaya Publications 2003

(2005 Winner of *EPIC* Award for Single Title/Mainstream)

Progressions

Desertion

It was Saturday morning tea time before Vanessa realized

something was different. She'd set out the breakfast things as usual, scouted round for laundry, brought in the paper and sprinkled cat food into the cat dish.

She sipped her tea, observed the empty chairs, the untouched breakfast, the unopened newspaper at the head of the table. She heard, in her head, footsteps, the meow of the cat, the rustle of the newspaper, the scrape of spoons, conversation. In reality, the only sound was her light breathing and the tick tick of the dining room clock.

Outside was all bright sunshine and blue skies, the same as yesterday. The chink of Waitamata Harbor visible through the lounge window showed a huge container ship steaming up the channel. Auckland, New Zealand's 'City of Sails' was certainly living up to its name that day. White yachts bobbed around the container ship, like icing peaks surrounding a wedding cake.

Wedding cakes, today of all days? Vanessa let her gaze be drawn toward the bland facades of the high rise buildings and the red and blue pulsing city lights, winking on-off, on-off, on-off. Just the same as yesterday. The day was the same. The city was the same. But she was different.

Because they had gone, all of them – husband, children. She looked around. Even the cat was gone.

A bubble of laughter rose to her throat. It was funny. Funny! Her life: Comedy of the week.

'Stuff you, Mum. We're off. Thanks for the last twenty years and all that. See you.'

When had the first one gone? Why hadn't she noticed? It had been Brent. The eldest, as it should be. Heading off on the great OE. She hadn't noticed his absence much because of the other two. Demanding daughter, Debbie, loud son, Mark. The house had still been full of their friends and noise and movement. She hadn't really noticed when Brent was no longer there.

Now the other two had gone off to join their elder sibling.

Off. The hysterical laughter was reaction. She was probably suffering from 'empty nest syndrome'. Every emotion had a name these days. Nothing was sacred anymore. You couldn't have a good cry without family, friends and health care specialists giving it a three letter name and suggesting that you take this vitamin supplement or that herbal extract. She had bottles of such things in a cupboard somewhere. Or perhaps she was just feeling her forty-four years?

Vanessa put down her cup and tried to ignore the trembling of her fingers. So, all her children had gone. Left home. Departed the nest. Flown the coop. She would just have to accept it. No doubt they would be back when they needed something.

The thought had her pushing back her chair and getting quickly to her feet. She didn't want them back! She was glad they had gone. Glad! Relief washed through her in a great wave. No more three loads of washing every day, no more ferrying children to hockey, rugby or basketball games, no more suffering teenage parties, no more huge dentist's bills, no more endless cooking of endless meals.

She was free! Vanessa wanted to climb up on top of the table and kick plates and cereal about the room. She actually had one foot on her chair about to do that, when a flood of guilt attacked her. She must be mad! She must be having one of those pre-menopausal breakdowns she had read about, (which she could possibly find some vitamin supplement or herbal extract to combat).

She caught sight of her reflection in the mirror on the opposite wall and thought, in some surprise, 'Yes, I do look mad!' Her shoulders were hunched and her grey-green eyes were staring. Her short honey blond hair was all scrunched up, too. She had forgotten to brush it that morning. What with everything.

She plumped back onto her chair, looked toward the head of the table at the unopened newspaper, and she faced the thing she had been trying not to think about all morning.

Ron. Her husband. He had gone, too.

Vanessa recalled the pathetic little one sided conversation of the previous night.

"You don't really mind do you, Van, if I shove off?"

Worm.

"We've reached the end of the line with our marriage, Van. Haven't we? Honestly, I mean. You know, past our 'use by' date."

Worm.

"Er...well." He pulled at his double-breasted suit jacket, which he'd taken to wearing of late to disguise an expanding paunch. How Vanessa disliked those dark-gray, pinstriped suits. They were so much the uniform of the successful accountant and smacked of Ron's expansive, middle-aged lifestyle, which had become more and more nothing at all to do with her. The suits made him look shorter than ever; and she'd always been annoyed by the

fact that Ron was short, hardly much above her own five

foot four inches.

"You'll have the house, Van." He puffed out his chest to look

important and his flat grey eyes actually met hers for a second.

"There's no argument there. I've a bit put aside. Not much,"

hastily. "But enough to set us, I mean, enough."

Worm. As if she hadn't guessed?

"You'll be all right. You've got your job at the shop, friends"

– vaguely – "And there's Debbie. She's a good daughter to you."

Blind worm.

"Well, I'll just get a few things." Sounds came to her of

furtive rustlings in the wardrobe for shirts and trousers. "You

don't mind if I take this suitcase, do you, Van? It's quite a good

size for a...I mean, for me."

He'd almost said 'for a man' and she'd nearly laughed at

that.

"Well, that's that, then." Catches clinking closed, unmusical, dull. Final. He brushed a hand through his thinning mousy hair. Vanessa was sure he had copied that mannerism from a film he'd seen somewhere. Not with her, of course.

"You've been good about this, Van." A guilty flare of color stained his sallow cheeks. He gave a little dart of his tongue, like a dog waiting for a tidbit. Thank God he'd stopped at pecking her cheek. She couldn't have borne it.

"Well, I'll be off now, Van. I'll keep in touch...the children and...Well, goodbye." He backed hastily from the room.

She had listened to him thumping down the hallway and out to the car, the car starting up and driving away down the road. Then...silence.

Vanessa turned her gaze from the unopened newspaper. She forced the laughter back down her throat. She couldn't laugh. People would say she was mad. *Your children left, your husband left and you, laughed*? Yes, they would say she was mad. Prescribe something stronger than vitamin supplements and herbal extracts for her. Lock her up in a place with pale green walls.

Best to appear calm. She poured herself another cup of tea, calmly, reached for the newspaper and opened it, calmly, at 'news of the world'.

The Beginning

Always begin with a change in the protagonist's life. Something has happened and this forces the protagonist to re-think their life. They *have* to act. Sometimes this is in the form of dramatic action – a fight for their lives. Often it's a case of moving from their comfortable environment, changing their job, or learning to accept and live with whatever change has happened.

The story opens with the protagonist, Vanessa, reviewing her domestic situation. The reader is privy to Vanessa's thoughts and innermost feelings and reactions as she takes stock of the situation and slowly absorbs the fact that the life she has known for many years is changed forever.

Vanessa sees her changed circumstances as funny. 'Her life: Comedy of the week.' While she recognizes her 'hysterical laughter' is reaction, underneath she knows she'll have to accept the situation.

'Every emotion had a name these days. Nothing was sacred anymore. You couldn't have a good cry without family, friends and health care specialists giving it a three letter name and suggesting that you take this vitamin supplement or that herbal extract. She had bottles of such things in a cupboard somewhere.'

This suggests Vanessa's use of such remedies in the past. Once, she might have had 'a good cry'. But none of it worked then and won't now. She is used to finding a bottle of 'herbal extracts' to combat her emotions, or suppressing them altogether.

When she realizes her children are not coming back – or only when they want something – she feels 'a great wave of relief' at the freedom from domestic chores. 'She wanted to climb up on top of the table and kick plates and cereal about the room.'

It's here that Vanessa thinks she might be mad or suffering from 'one of those pre-menopausal breakdowns she had read about'. She plumps back down onto her chair and forces herself to face the fact of her husband's departure – a thing she had been ignoring until that moment.

The scene, a flashback to the previous evening's one-sided conversation between Vanessa and her husband, Ron, gives further insight into Vanessa's marriage. She suppressed her feelings during those years, and must suppress them now, even her laughter. 'Best to appear calm,' she decides.

She reaches for Ron's newspaper and opens it, calmly, at 'news of the world'; thereby relegating her own changed circumstances or news to its rightful unimportant place.

This might be considered Vanessa's platform or stance, how she will face the future. She'll accept things, keep her emotions to herself and carry on regardless. This will form a barrier, act as her buffer against things to come, and help hide her true feelings.

The story will show how Vanessa copes with, and comes to terms with her new life, what she learns along the way. The reader has the pleasure of sharing her journey.

Opening Chapters

Study the opening chapters of other novels and examine how the writer presents the protagonist/s and their problem/s.

The first chapters often pose the most trouble for writers. I re-work and change my first chapters many times. It's part of writing.

Exercise Ten

- Why not begin the first chapter of your own novel? This might involve several attempts but don't let that stop you.

- Take your time to collect your thoughts and ideas.

- Consider your theme/s. What things are important to you?

- Read other novels in your chosen genre to give you inspiration.

- Find inspiring photographs.

- Make a rough plot outline using mind maps, keywords and sentences.

- Choose a title, one that says something about the book if possible.

To Re-Cap What We Covered in Chapter Eight

* Novels

The Opening Chapter of My Novel *Progressions*

* The Beginning

Always begin with a change in the protagonist's life. Something has happened and this forces the protagonist to re-think their life. They *have* to act. Sometimes this is in the form of dramatic action – a fight for their lives. Often it's a case of moving from their comfortable environment, changing their job, or learning to accept and live with whatever change has happened.

* Opening Chapters

Study the opening chapters of other novels and examine how the writer presents the protagonist/s and their problem/s.

* Exercise Ten

Why not begin the first chapter of your own novel?

9 HOW TO USE SETTING AS A CHARACTER

In Chapter Nine we examine how setting works as a character in a Young Adult novel, and how to use language that suits your characters. We look at how to use descriptive words and sentences to add tension to your scene.

Never open with a long, lengthy, wordy paragraph. The glorious sunset/sunrise, the wonderful flowering shrubs/trees/garden, or the busy tangle of a motorway, need to include your characters. Incorporate their thoughts and actions into your scenes.

This is their stage; make every prop work.

In the following opening chapter of my YA novel, *Timeboy Book One: Gondwana Jupiter Publishing NZ Ltd* 2013, study how the opening introduces the main characters, and how the setting works to create tension.

Timeboy Book One: Gondwana

Chapter One: The Quarry

The boys reached the quarry as the first of the sun's rays struck the yellow clay.

Matt stopped, puffing hard. The summer morning was warm, yet something about the place gave him the creeps. Not a bird or animal squeaked.

"Ok, D. Show me the footprint. And it'd better be worth getting up this early for." He scowled at his nine year old foster brother.

D gave him a fierce look and pushed past. "I know you don't believe me, Matt, but I saw it! Clear as anything." He took off, running through the bowl of the quarry, his shoes slap-slapping on the dry clay. "It's over here." He stopped, his thin shoulders heaving. "There!" He pointed to the ground, and his young voice quivered with excitement. "There it is, just as I said!"

Matt followed more slowly. He hadn't believed D's claim about the giant footprint. D was always making up stories. He was a pest. Matt couldn't believe he'd given up his Sunday morning sleep-in to investigate. Orange and PJ had thought him crazy to even consider looking at the thing.

Matt wished he hadn't told them about D's footprint. How they'd laughed! Orange had goofed around, pretending to be Bigfoot pulling faces and making revolting noises. Matt remembered how he and PJ had rolled about in stitches. PJ had told practically everyone. The whole school was laughing! Now Matt felt awful, and disloyal. He shouldn't have said anything. D was so intense, so caught up in his fantasy world.

Matt hadn't wanted a kid foster brother, especially one as

weird as D.

"You'd better not be making this up," he'd said to him last night.

"I'm not, Matt. I swear. You've gotta come and see it. Please!"

Matt had been about to tell him to shove off, but D's pleading gray eyes had stopped him. That, and the guilty feeling he should be making more of an effort with D.

"I know D's a bit strange, but he's had it hard," his mother had said from that first day, nearly a year ago now. "Try and make friends with him. He's very good with animals."

If only his mother hadn't said *that*. Animals and Matt were a sore point. Unfortunately. Being the only son of two farm-loving people and being less than interested in farming and animals himself led to major problems in his life.

D's arrival had only made things worse.

"Look, Matt!" D dropped to the ground and sprawled out on

his stomach, propping his chin on his hands. "Check out the size of that print!"

Matt looked. He didn't know what he'd expected. A hawk's footprint? Or maybe a rabbit's paw? Or a cows hoof print, enlarged out of proportion as the animal had slid in the wet clay? What he wasn't prepared for was the large rounded footprint. It made him take a step back. He blinked and looked again. The print was still there; uncanny, too big. He couldn't make it out at all.

D's face was inches from the dried mud puddle, his gaze fixed on the footprint.

Matt fought away another shiver – and the urge to pull D away. "Probably a rabbit," he said.

"It's not a rabbit." D shook his head. "Rabbits only weigh about half a kilo. This animal's gotta weigh a hundred times that." D's voice rose on the 'hundred.' He inched closer. "Nah. Gotta be heavier than even that. *Way* heavier."

Matt wanted to swear, but he knew D was right. D was a walking encyclopedia when it came to animals and birds. Matt glanced around again, noting the silence of the quarry for the second time. The macrocarpa tree that had been blown down last winter lay like something beheaded, its twisted roots clotted with lumps of dry clay. All down one side of the sun-silvered trunk the cattle had rubbed against it until it was worn smooth. He wanted to run his hand along the polished wood, to reconnect with the familiar.

Something moved then, off to his right. His gaze swung to catch the movement, a flash of dark gray hide, touched with strange markings.

Goose bumps crawled over his skin. Instinct told him it wasn't a cow or a bullock or even a wild pig. He knew what *they* looked like. Dave on the next block had just got in a few Murray Greys; but it wasn't one of those either. The hide had been too gray, too tough-looking, too strange.

His gaze came back to D, who was still sprawled on the ground, mesmerized by the footprint, and oblivious to his surroundings. Matt dragged in a breath. "Let's get out of here." The words were out before he could stop them. What was the matter with him, allowing shadows to spook him? If only he had some of D's affinity with animals.

"Why can't you be more like D?" Dad was always saying these days with 'that' tone in his voice that always made Matt feel like a loser. "D's got a great way with animals."

D hadn't heard him anyway. "Come and look closer, Matt." A thin arm beckoned Matt forward.

Matt scowled. He didn't want to 'look closer'. That would make the footprint real. Then he'd have to think what had made it.

"Yeah. I can see it." He tried for an offhand tone. "Come on, D. It's just an old rabbit got his foot caught in a possum trap and it grew all deformed. Maybe it's even a possum, or one of the cattle. The cattle come through here all the time."

At that, D looked up sharply. He pushed to his feet. "It isn't a rabbit or a possum, Matt." He shook his head and his tangled black curls jangled. "And it's not cattle." He glared. "Cattle have hooves, Matt," he said as if Matt was stupid. "Not feet like that. That's a soft footed animal." His gaze swung back to the footprint, and he heaved in a breath. "It's none of them. It's a…?" He swallowed and tried again. "I think it's a… At least I'm pretty sure it's a…?"

A crash off to one side of the quarry had them both jumping. Matt looked for the gray thing. His skin went cold again. D must have felt something, too, for his eyes widened.

The whole quarry seemed to hesitate, to hold its breath.

The noise came again, followed by a shallow rumble that rose at the end in a weird squeak. No rabbit. No possum. Nothing Matt had ever heard before.

He saw D's eyes widen further, but when a silly grin spread

over his features, and his head started turning this way and that as he searched for the thing that had made the noise, Matt's blood ran cold.

By the time he got his act together, D was already off and sprinting toward the sound.

Language

Use language that suits your characters: shove off, goofed around, check out, way heavier, feel like a loser, yeah

Action Words

Use verbs and action words: struck, squeaked, scowled, rolled, dropped, sprawled, shiver, slotted, rubbed, dragged

Description

Use descriptive words and sentences that add tension to your scene:

The first of the sun's rays struck the yellow clay.

The place gave him the creeps.

Not a bird or an animal squeaked.

The silence of the quarry.

The tree lay 'like something beheaded'.

The whole quarry seemed to hesitate, to hold its breath.

To reconnect with the familiar.

Sun-silvered trunk.

Pretending to be Bigfoot.

Weird squeak.

Tough-looking.

Contrast

Each character views their surroundings through different eyes.

D is excited.

His thin voice quivered with excitement.

'You gotta come and see it. Please!'

'Check out the size of that print!'

His gaze was 'mesmerized' by the footprint.

A silly grin spread over his face.

Matt sees the quarry differently.

'The place gave him the creeps.'

'He couldn't believe he'd given up his Sunday morning sleep-in to investigate the footprint.'

The footprint is 'uncanny'.

Goose bumps crawl over his skin.

He doesn't want to take a closer look at the footprint.

He wants to 'get out of there'.

His blood 'runs cold'.

This clash of personalities adds an extra dimension to the story – the *internal* problem for the characters to solve. The *external* problem is the footprint. To whom does it belong?

Children's Picture Books

Before we leave beginnings, let's examine the beginning of two of my children's picture books.

The following examples are from my picture books, *Sebastian's Tail Penguin Group (NZ)* 2008, and *Jossie's New Home Jupiter Publishing NZ Ltd* 2012

Sebastian's Tail

'Sebastian the rat was born without a tail. So he set out to find one.'

This introduces the protagonist, states his problem, and shows how he intends to solve the problem.

Jossie's New Home

'Jossie the Jersey cow was tired of living in a paddock. So she went looking for a new home.'

Once again this introduces the protagonist, states her problem, and shows how she intends to solve the problem.

Children's picture books use few words so there isn't time for long lengthy introductions. The writer needs to jump straight into the story and stay there.

Make every word count!

A Chapter Book Beginning

Study the beginning of my first chapter book for children, *The Giant Greglusam Jupiter Publishing NZ Ltd* 2014

The Giant Greglusam

Something washed up on the beach.

Samuel and Greg found it early one morning on the last day of the school holidays.

"What is it?" Greg crouched on the sand for a closer look.

"Looks weird." Samuel spun his hat brim to the back of his head and cautiously dropped down beside Greg. The thing *was* weird. Like nothing he'd seen before; bigger than a large garden pot and rounded and sort of lumpy looking with an outer dirty brown crust. He couldn't stop a shiver.

If only he could lose this being scared of everything? Ever since the 'bad time', months ago, when his world had changed forever, Samuel had been scared. He hadn't told anyone of his feelings, especially not his mother. She was scared, too. She spent all her time watching his baby sister, Jasmine. And the look on her face scared Samuel more than anything.

Now he was scared of some stupid lumpy thing on the beach.

External and Internal Problems

The story will show how Samuel copes with 'the weird thing' and the 'bad time'.

Again we have the external problem – the weird thing; and the internal problem – the 'bad time'. Both are resolved at the end.

To Re-Cap What we Covered in Chapter Nine

* How to Use Setting as a Character

Always incorporate your character's thoughts and actions into your scenes.

This is their stage; make every prop work.

* The First Chapter of *Timeboy Book One: Gondwana*

* Language

Use the language your characters use.

* Action Words

Use verbs more often.

* Description

Use descriptive words and sentences that add tension to your

scene.

* Contrast

Each character views their surroundings through different eyes.

* Children's Picture Books

The first line in two children's picture books.

* A Chapter Book

The opening paragraphs of my chapter book for children, *The Giant Greglusam.*

* External and Internal Problems

The external problem – the weird thing; and the internal problem – the 'bad time'.

10 THE FINISHED PRODUCT

In Chapter Ten I talk about the importance of finishing your book, and of how to cope with nervousness at this stage. There are sections on self-editing, finding an editor, publishing your book, and the Top Twenty-Five Points in *Take Heart & Write*.

Finish Your Work

This is the most important piece of writing advice I can give you. Don't give up half-way through or near the end because you decide your book is not perfect.

Forget 'perfect' and think 'finish'.

It's natural to have an attack of nerves at this stage, and many writers do – including me. You've spent weeks, maybe months on your writing project and now you're over it! It doesn't read right, it's not what you want, it doesn't work, you hate it.

A lot of creative people are never completely satisfied with their work. This is another fear we must learn to put aside and dig deep for the courage to finish.

You've had the courage to get this far, continue on that last bit – sometimes the longest part of the journey. You might be fighting writer fatigue, deadlines and any number of a dozen irritating glitches.

They are only glitches; don't allow them to grow bigger. Keep forging ahead, line by line, page by page, chapter by chapter until you can finally write 'the end'.

You *will* finish. It's only a matter of time.

When you can honestly say you've given it your best shot and you've written from the heart then your book *is* finished. Well, *almost*! You've completed what's known in the writing world as the 'rough draft' or the 'first draft'.

It's time for the next stage; self-editing.

Self-Editing

Now is the time to remove your writer's hat and put on your editor's hat, to examine your work with an analytical eye. Be honest!

- Put your book aside for several days or a week, then read through from the beginning, as if you're reading it for the first time.

- Read your book aloud. You'll soon hear those words that clang, that sound out of place, the sentences you know you can write with more clarity.

- What are your favorite parts? Make a list of the good points. Where you've explained yourself clearly and concisely – if you've written a non-fiction book – or where your characters shine, if you've written fiction.

- How does your book read now?

- What parts need more work?

- What do *you* want to change?

- How easy/difficult is this to achieve?

- Can you break the bigger bits into manageable bites?

- It might seem a lot of work, but how many hours are needed?

- Give yourself a time limit – perhaps two weeks. You don't want to be still editing in six weeks' time no further ahead.

- Don't keep on 'editing forever' or you'll never finish or be happy with it.

- Books can always be changed/added to later.

An Editing Session

How the above section looked before editing.

It's time to remove your writer's hat and put on your editor's hat, to look at your work with an analytical eye.

Put your book aside f for several days or a week, then read through it from the beginning, as if you were reading it fro the first time. Read your book aloud. You'll soon hear those words that clang, that sound out of place, those sentences you know you can write with more clarity.

Again

What do you like about your book? Make a list of the good points, where you explained yourself clearly and concisly – if you've written a non-fiction book – or where your characters shine – if you've written fiction.

How does it read now? W

What parts can you see need changing?

What parts do you want to change?

How easy/difficlt will this be?

Break the bigger bits down into manageable 'bites.'

Give yourself a time limit so that you won't be still there in six weeks time no further ahead.

Is it really that difficult to change the bigger bits?

It might seem like a lot of work, but honestly, how many hors are needed?

Dpn Don't keep on editing forever or you will never finish be happy with it.

Morst books that are published can always be changed/added to later.

Accept that u you witll be better nest time.

Granted most of the mistakes are typos, but I wanted to change some of the sentences, and add things, to say it in the best way I could.

How have I done? Do the changes improve the piece?

It's all about doing the best you can.

The Last Lap

At last you've finished your book! Along with the relief and satisfaction this brings, there'll be fresh fears as you wonder if you've got it right, or if you've done enough self-editing?

Another round of patience is required as you do a final reading.

Look for:

- Spelling mistakes

- Punctuation mistakes

- Misused words

- Clumsy sentences

- Long, lengthy, wordy paragraphs

- Waffle of any kind

- Repetition of words in the same paragraph/section

- Run a final spell check

When you feel your book is the best you can make it, find an editor. No matter how many times you read through your work, you'll always miss spelling mistakes, and many other errors. An experienced editor will find these mistakes, and offer valuable advice on how to improve your book.

When you receive your book back, you'll be amazed at the things you've missed! Don't be dismayed, accept the expert advice and make the changes. Your book will be much improved by that professional polish.

Your Book is Ready for Publishing

Now, your book is ready for publishing. This can be both exciting and terrifying! You're about to launch your book. People will read it. Some will like it, some won't. Don't lose your nerve now and decide you don't want to publish your book because the idea is too scary. *Take Heart*! Have confidence in what you've written.

This is your voice; like no other.

If you're worried about what people will think – a genuine fear for most of us – invite several people to read your book and give you a fair review. If you ask family and close friends to read your book they'll likely tell you 'it's great!' as they won't want to hurt your feelings.

Be careful before you allow people to read your book. If you don't receive positive feedback, then you'll probably be so upset you won't publish your book. What you need is a fair review or someone who will comment on your book in a fair and helpful manner.

Whatever you decide, remain true to your convictions. Don't

allow doubts to sway you from your course at this stage – to

publish your book.

Whether you've decided to self-publish or publish through

traditional channels, publishing can take time. Be prepared for an

enjoyable, rewarding and sometimes tough experience – rather

like the writing journey itself.

Top Twenty-Five Points in *Take Heart & Write*

1) First Fear Barrier

- Congratulations! You've driven past that dreaded first fear

  barrier. Give a jaunty 'toot'.

- You're now well on your way along the writing highway

  and traveling at your own pace.

- Don't let 'dead ends' and 'wrong-way' signs deter you.

  Steer clear of 'road works' and 'traffic jams'.

- Hold a steady 'writing course'.

2) Courage

- Courage is the opposite of cowardice. It is bravery, guts, daring, nerve, audacity, pluck, valor, and the ability to act on one's convictions.
- You have every one of these capabilities. Sometimes you need to dig deep to find them, to allow them to rise to the forefront of your mind, to remind you that you *can* achieve whatever you set out to do.
- We *all* have courage. Repeat the word 'courage', to yourself like a mantra; courage, courage, courage!
- Metaphorically, pin the badge of courage to your chest every day before you write and there will be no stopping you.

3) Patience

- Cultivate patience.

- Don't give in to impatience, or worry there's too much to learn and that you'll never find the time, energy or the ability to absorb it all.

- You *will* achieve all you set out to do.

- Patience.

4) Writer Zone/Mood and Time Management

- Relax and get into your writer zone/mood.

- Find time in your schedule for your writing. There is always spare time if we search.

- Use your most creative hours to write.

- Set yourself realistic and achievable goals.

5) The Power of Reward and Encouragement

- Reward yourself when you complete each writing exercise. Rewarding yourself and taking pleasure in your writing achievements is important.

- Never underestimate the power of reward and encouragement in the creative field.

- Ask your family/friends/work colleagues to offer encouragement; don't forget to thank them for their support.

6) Practice and Determination

- Practice is one of the best things you can do to improve your writing.

- Make time for practice writing sessions as often as you can, every day if possible.

- Build up your word bank.

- Write a 'snap shot' scene once a week.

- Set yourself a writing challenge.

7) Knowledge and Learning

- Make learning a lifelong apprenticeship.

- We learn by doing. It's a simple formula but effective.

- Knowledge is knowledge for life.

- Join your local writing group. Interaction with other keen writers is great for your writing soul and a terrific way to keep you motivated. It's also a good way to meet and make new friends – once a writing friend, always a writing friend.

8) Be a Reader

- If you want to be a writer, you need to be a reader.

- If you've chosen to write in a particular genre, it pays to read what's being written and published in that genre. Search out the bestsellers in your local library, bookshop or on-line.

9) Publish Your Work

- Publish your writing from the beginning – on-line, for your family and friends, or with traditional publishing houses.

- The past is the past; it's a new beginning in the writing world.

- Be excited; there's never been a better time to write.

10) Focus

- Learn to block out distractions and background noises to focus on your writing so it becomes your center of attention, your 'focal point'.

11) Truth and Honesty

- Be truthful with your writer self. Regard your writing with honest eyes.

- As you progress you'll learn to recognize what works and what doesn't.

12) Keep Persevering

- Is that golden crown of perseverance still sitting upon your head? Don't let anything dislodge it. Keep adjusting when necessary.

- Perseverance.

13) The Power of Words and Inspiration

- Use keywords.

- Never be stuck for words, inspiration is everywhere. You will never run out of ideas. Be inquisitive.

- Record your ideas so you don't lose or forget them.

14) Productivity

- Some days are more productive than others; that's the way of writing. Don't be disillusioned by the less productive days.

- Keep writing and remember your book is building word by word, sentence by sentence, chapter by chapter.

- Every writing day is productive. Your subconscious mind will still be working long after you've put aside your pen, or switched off your computer.

15) Tricks of the Trade and Safety Nets for Your Ideas

- Take a writing break. Make a coffee or tea. Walk around the house, your office. Let your subconscious mind find the right words and ideas. It works.

- End your writing session in the middle of a paragraph or scene so you can continue next time without hesitation.

- Use keywords, headings and mind maps to record ideas for further chapters/scenes/characters.

16) Inner Belief/How to Fight Negativity

- There's always someone prepared to put you off; ignore them.

- Replace negativity with positive, encouraging thoughts. Every positive, encouraging thought is a step up, a literal and figurative push along your writing path.

- *Believe* in yourself.

17) Point of View

- We don't always have to write about ourselves or from our own experiences – our POV.

- POV can be confusing. It's wise to stay in one person's POV to avoid confusing the reader.

- Begin a new chapter from another character's POV.

18) Show, Don't Tell

- Don't *tell* the reader how your character is feeling. *Show* your character's emotions through action and let the reader decide for themselves.

- Describe your character through the eyes of another character – always the best way in my opinion.

- **19) Find Your Way of Writing**

- There are no rules in writing, no 'right' way to write, just different ways.

- Find *your* way.

- Use *everything* to your advantage, including time and place.

20) Our Writer's Soul

- In every piece of writing a part of the writer is revealed, our writer's soul, if you will. It doesn't matter if we write fiction or non-fiction; a part of who we are is

unconsciously revealed.

- This is what makes our stories moving and more intense.

  We are sharing our own/our character's innermost

  emotions with our reader.

21) Theme/Plot

- Theme is what the story is about.
- Plot is what happens in the story.

22) Finish Your Work

- This is the most important piece of writing advice I can

  give you. Don't give up half-way through or near the end

  because you decide your book is not perfect.
- Forget 'perfect' and think 'finish'.

23) Self-Editing/Finding an Editor

- Write first; edit later.

- Examine your work with an analytical eye. Be honest.

- An experienced editor will find mistakes you've missed, and offer valuable advice on how to improve your book.

24) Your Book is Ready for Publishing

- This can be both exciting and terrifying! You're about to launch your book. Don't lose your nerve now and decide you don't want to publish your book because the idea is too scary. *Take Heart!* Have confidence in what you've written.

- This is your voice; like no other.

25) Hold Fast to Your Dreams

- Your dream was to write. If you've followed the exercises presented in *Take Heart & Write*, and invented your own, you are achieving your dream.

My Last Word – The Journey of the Pen

Writers have inspired, enlightened and championed man from the beginning. Famous orations move millions. Armies march at 'calls to action'. Poets make us weep at their lyrical masterpieces.

To be part of the writing world is a privilege to cherish.

As writers, we start with a blank canvas and an idea – then we pick up our pens and the journey begins. A journey that can be both exhilarating and exhausting.

But isn't that the way of most journeys?

There's the thrill of starting out, followed by the trials and tribulations of travel.

You experience the excitement of arriving at your destination, and the eagerness to explore a new place. The exhilaration of being on holiday gives way to a flat feeling that your holiday is ending. Then the nostalgia of returning home rises to boost you on your homeward journey. Finally, you realize your memories will stay with you forever.

Writing a short story or a novel is challenging.

The only way you'll know what you can achieve is by taking up that challenge with confidence and courage.

Happy writing everyone!

ABOUT THE AUTHOR

Judy Lawn has been writing for thirty years. Her ideas for her short stories, picture books and novels come from her love of animals and nature, and a childhood spent exploring the countryside and beaches of New Zealand's North Island.

A keen fisher, Judy's first published short story was a fishing yarn, *Sam's Kingie*.

Other short stories have been published in various magazines, including *New Zealand Woman's Weekly* and *Australian/New Zealand Woman's Day*, and *Takahe Magazine*.

Judy's first novel *Progressions* won the 2005 Epic Award for best Single Title/Mainstream.

Her first children's picture books was *The Shrimp Who Wanted to be Pink, Reed Publishing (NZ) Ltd* 2003. *Sebastian's Tail, Penguin Group (NZ)* was published in 2008.

Judy lives in Whangaparaoa where the many beautiful beaches and parklands provide inspiration for her stories.

A long-held dream of starting her own publishing company came to fruition in 2011, with the launch of *Jupiter Publishing NZ Ltd*. The company ran until the end of July, 2015.

To learn more about Judy, and to read excerpts from her books, and the short story, *Sam's Kingie*, visit her website: www.judylawn.com